GREAT MILITARY LEADERS
of the 20TH Century

DOUGLAS MACARTHUR
MAO ZEDONG
GEORGE S. PATTON
JOHN J. PERSHING
ERWIN J.E. ROMMEL
H. NORMAN SCHWARZKOPF

GREAT MILITARY LEADERS
of the 20TH Century

H. NORMAN SCHWARZKOPF

TIM McNEESE

INTRODUCTION BY
CASPAR W. WEINBERGER

SERIES CONSULTING EDITOR
EARLE RICE JR.

CHELSEA HOUSE
PUBLISHERS
A Haights Cross Communications Company

Philadelphia

FRONTIS: H. Norman Schwarzkopf at ease with his tank troops in Operation Desert Storm. Saudi Arabia, January 12, 1991.

CHELSEA HOUSE PUBLISHERS

VP, NEW PRODUCT DEVELOPMENT Sally Cheney
DIRECTOR OF PRODUCTION Kim Shinners
CREATIVE MANAGER Takeshi Takahashi
MANUFACTURING MANAGER Diann Grasse

STAFF FOR H. NORMAN SCHWARZKOPF

EXECUTIVE EDITOR Lee Marcott
PRODUCTION ASSISTANT Megan Emery
PICTURE RESEARCHER Noelle Nardone
SERIES & COVER DESIGNER Takeshi Takahashi
LAYOUT 21st Century Publishing and Communications, Inc.

©2004 by Chelsea House Publishers,
a subsidiary of Haights Cross Communications.
All rights reserved. Printed in China.

A Haights Cross Communications ✈ Company

http://www.chelseahouse.com

First Printing

1 3 5 7 9 8 6 4 2

Library of Congress Cataloging-in-Publication Data

McNeese, Tim.
    H. Norman Schwarzkopf / by Tim McNeese.
      p. cm. -- (Great military leaders of the 20th century)
Summary: Reviews the life and battles of General "Stormin'" Norman
Schwarzkopf, who commanded American troops in the Persian Gulf
War of 1991. Includes bibliographical references and index.
    ISBN 0-7910-7406-4 (Hardcover)
    1. Schwarzkopf, H. Norman, 1934---Juvenile literature. 2. Generals--
United States--Biography--Juvenile literature. 3. United States. Army--
Biography--Juvenile literature. 4. Persian Gulf War, 1991--Juvenile
literature. [1. Schwarzkopf, H. Norman, 1934- 2. Generals. 3. Persian
Gulf War, 1991.] I. Title. II. Series.
E840.5.S39M36 2003
355'.0092--dc21
                                                            2003007283

TABLE OF CONTENTS

INTRODUCTION

by Caspar W. Weinberger

At a time when it is ever more apparent that the world will need skilled and bold military leaders, it is both appropriate and necessary that school history courses include studies of great military leaders.

Democracies, for the most part, are basically not greatly interested in military leadership or military matters in general. Fortunately, in the United States we have sufficient interest and volunteers for military service so that we can maintain and staff a very strong military with volunteers—people who want to serve.

That is very fortunate indeed for us. Volunteers and those who decide of their own free will that they want to be in the military are, generally speaking, easier to train, and to retain in the services, and their morale is markedly higher than that of conscripts. Furthermore, the total effect of a draft, based on our Vietnam experience, can be very bad—indeed it can polarize the country as a whole.

One of the best ways of ensuring that we will continue to have enough volunteers in the future is to study the great accomplishments of our past military leaders—the small group of leaders and others who contributed so much to our past greatness and our present strength.

Not all of these leaders have been Americans, but the

example that all of them set are well worth studying in our schools. Of the six military leaders chosen by Chelsea House's "Great Military Leaders of the 20th Century," I had the privilege of serving under and with two.

In World War II, after two years of volunteer service in the infantry at home and in the Pacific, I was transferred from the 41st Infantry Division then in New Guinea, to General Douglas MacArthur's intelligence staff in Manila, in the Philippines. One of my assignments was to prepare drafts of the general's daily communiqué to other theatre commanders around the world. This required seeing all of the major military cable and intelligence information, and digesting the most important items for his daily report to the other war theatres of the world. It also required a familiarity with our plans to carry the war to the enemy as soon as sufficient strength had been transferred to our theatre from Europe.

The invasion of Japan toward which all the planning was aiming would have been a very difficult and costly operation. Most of the tentative plans called for landing our force on one of the southern Japanese islands, and another force on Honshu, north of Tokyo.

We know that Japan's troops would have fought fiercely and very skillfully once their homeland was invaded. In fact, all of our plans forecast that we would lose virtually all of the first two U.S. divisions that landed. That was one of the main reasons that President Harry Truman concluded we had to use the atomic bomb. That ended the war, and all landings taken in Japan were peaceful and unopposed.

Many years later, when I was secretary of defense under President Ronald Reagan, a part of my duties was to recommend generals and admirals for various U.S. and NATO regional commands. Fulfilling this duty led me to interview several possible candidates for the post of commander in chief of our Central Command, which had jurisdiction over our many military activities in the Middle East.

My strong recommendation, accepted by the president, was that he name General H. Norman Schwarzkopf to lead the Central Command. A short time later, General Schwarzkopf led our forces in that region to the great military victory of the Gulf War.

General MacArthur and General Schwarzkopf shared many of the same qualities. Both were very experienced army officers tested by many widely different conditions all over the world. Both were calm, resolute, and inspirational leaders. Both were superb military planners and developers of complex and very large-scale military operations. Both achieved great military successes; both had the best interest of all our troops at heart; and both were leaders in the best sense of the word. They both had the ability and skills necessary to work with military and civilian leaders of our allies and friends in all parts of the globe.

It is vitally important for our future as a democracy, a superpower and a country whose strengths have helped save freedom and peace, that our children and our schools know far more about these leaders and countless others like them who serve the cause of peace with freedom so well and so faithfully. Their lives and the lives of others like them will be a great inspiration for us and for later generations who need to know what America at its best can accomplish.

The other military leaders whose lives are presented in this series include a German, General Erwin Rommel, and the former Communist China leader, Mao Zedong.

General Rommel won many preliminary battles in the desert war of World War II before losing the decisive battle of El Alamein. He had to develop and execute his tactics for desert fighting under conditions not previously experienced by him or his troops. He also became one of the masters of the art of tank warfare.

Mao Zedong had to train, develop, arm, and deploy huge numbers of Chinese soldiers to defeat the organized and experienced forces of Chiang Kai-shek's Nationalist government. He accomplished this and, in comparatively short time, won the military victories that transformed his country.

Both of these generals had to learn, very quickly, the new tactics needed to cope with rapidly changing conditions. In short, they had to be flexible, inventive, and willing and able to fight against larger opposing forces and in unfamiliar environments.

This whole series demonstrates that great military success requires many of the qualities and skills required for success in other fields of endeavor. Military history is indeed a vital part of the whole story of mankind, and one of the best ways of studying that history is to study the lives of those who succeeded by their leadership in this vital field.

CASPAR W. WEINBERGER
CHAIRMAN, *FORBES* INC
MARCH 2003

★   ★   ★

CASPAR W. WEINBERGER was the fifteenth U.S. secretary of defense, serving under President Ronald Reagan from 1981 to 1987, longer than any previous defense secretary except Robert McNamara (served 1961–1968). Weinberger is also an author who has written books about his experiences in the Reagan administration and about U.S. military capabilities.

1

In His Father's Footsteps

On August 2, 1990, an angry Saddam Hussein, autocratic leader of the Middle Eastern nation of Iraq, ordered 100,000 troops into the heart of his southern neighbor, Kuwait. Through the early morning hours, as Iraqi tanks rumbled south following the superhighway of their oil-rich neighbor, helicopters flew Iraqi special forces into Kuwait City. The city fell quickly. The Kuwaiti army numbered no more than 20,000 men, no match for Saddam's seasoned soldiers, many of whom had seen action during Iraq's recently completed eight-year war with another of its neighbors, Iran. The emir (leader) of Kuwait, Sheikh Jaber al Ahmad al Sabah, was whisked from the royal palace and out of Kuwait City aboard a helicopter. The emir took refuge in Saudi Arabia, yet another neighboring country.

From the rooftop of the American embassy in Kuwait City, Major John Feeley, who had arrived in the city just days earlier, listened as explosions erupted across town. He watched Iraqi tanks roll through the streets. Fighter planes and helicopters struck hard at their targets. By satellite radio, he spoke to U.S. Central Command (CentCom) in Tampa, Florida, informing his superior that the Iraqis were occupying downtown Kuwait City. General H. Norman Schwarzkopf, CentCom commander, assessed the situation and picked up the receiver of a red phone. On a high-security direct line, he called General Colin Powell, chairman of the Joint Chiefs of Staff, and updated him on the Iraqi incursion. Powell told Schwarzkopf to prepare to brief President George H.W. Bush by the next day.

Over the following days, General Schwarzkopf became the focus of the American response to the Iraqi invasion of Kuwait. Iraqi control of Kuwait's oil was unacceptable to the Americans, who saw Saddam Hussein's aggression as unwarranted. When the three divisions of Iraqi Republican Guard forces turned farther south on Kuwaiti soil and began to mass along the border between Kuwait and Saudi Arabia, one of America's strongest allies in the region, Schwarzkopf and his superiors understood the need to move decisively. Kuwait had already fallen; Saudi Arabia must not.

Four days later, Schwarzkopf and Secretary of Defense Dick Cheney were in Saudi Arabia to meet with King Fahd, the ruler of the powerful Middle Eastern state, to discuss how to defend his kingdom and its oil resources. The meeting was crucial. The Saudi kingdom was conservative and rigorous in its support of Islam, the Muslim religion. The presence of a largely non-Muslim American force on Saudi soil would cause major disputes within the ranks of the Saudi royal family. It was General Schwarzkopf's responsibility to explain to the king the threat the Iraqis posed to his country. Should the American general fail in his efforts, Saudi Arabia would stand nearly defenseless in the face of a second round of Iraqi aggression.

The Americans arrived at the Saudi palace in Jidda, along the banks of the Red Sea, where the king usually spent his summers. The contingent rolled into the city in a fleet of Mercedes automobiles that had been provided by the king. On the afternoon of August 6, just four days after the Iraqi invasion of Kuwait, King Fahd ushered in the group of American representatives, including Schwarzkopf. Silk carpets of green and gold covered the floor. Flanked by several royal princes, the king rose to greet his guests. Only Secretary Cheney and General Schwarzkopf were to speak during the formal session. After Cheney spoke briefly to King Fahd, delivering greetings from President Bush, the secretary turned everyone's attention to General Schwarzkopf, the man best equipped to convey the urgency of the situation to the king. The moment was anxious and tense. In his mission to convince King Fahd to allow hundreds of thousands of American troops onto Saudi soil, the general knew that he had to succeed.

As Schwarzkopf approached the king, history was repeating itself. His father, General H. Norman Schwarzkopf, Sr., had advised another Middle Eastern leader, the shah of Iran, during World War II. Now, for a second time, the potential future of the Middle East hung on the words of another American general—and another Schwarzkopf. The younger Schwarzkopf, in fact, had been named for his father.

H. Norman Schwarzkopf, Jr., was born in Trenton, New Jersey, on August 22, 1934. Despite the fact that his father, Herbert Norman Schwarzkopf, Sr., hated the name "Herbert," he still gave it to his son. Norman Schwarzkopf, Sr., had attended the U.S. Military Academy at West Point, New York, and graduated in the class of 1917, just in time to be sent to serve in Europe during World War I. After the war, he was selected to be military police chief of an American-occupied town in Germany. This job eventually led Schwarzkopf, Sr., into police work when he returned home after his European tour of duty.

Young Schwarzkopf's mother was four years younger than his father. Born Ruth Bowman in 1900, she had been raised in the small West Virginia town of Bluefield, nestled in the Appalachian Mountains, "where as a girl she had made pocket money taking tourists up a mountain to look at the sunrise."[1] When Ruth left home, she moved to New Jersey, where she studied nursing and eventually took a job at a large hospital in Trenton. Later, wealthy families employed her as a private nurse.

Schwarzkopf, Sr., returned from Europe in 1921. He resigned his officer's commission immediately and returned to civilian life, but only briefly. That same year, the governor of New Jersey, Teddy Edwards, appointed Schwarzkopf as the first superintendent of the newly formed New Jersey State Police, with a rank of colonel. In fact, Schwarzkopf played a major role in organizing the force, selecting its first officers, and even designing the original state police uniform. Although Colonel Schwarzkopf was only 25 years old when he accepted his state police position, he "turned out to be a natural at the job: he loved every aspect of organizing the force, from setting up training schedules to . . . inventing exercises that would build morale."[2]

Throughout the 1920s and 1930s, Colonel Schwarzkopf ran his state police unit with the efficiency and discipline of a West Point graduate. He fought hard against Depression-era crime in his home state. New Jersey was a haven for bootleggers, people who smuggled alcohol despite the restrictions of Prohibition. Schwarzkopf, Sr., had been selected to head the state police precisely because he was an honest and tough law enforcement officer. While wearing a police uniform, he lived by the West Point motto: "Duty, Honor, Country."

H. Norman Schwarzkopf, Sr., returned from military service in Europe to become the superintendent of the New Jersey state police. He is seen here in his police uniform.

Norman Schwarzkopf, Sr., and Ruth Bowman met at a reception in Trenton in 1928. During the festivities, Norman asked Ruth if he could take her on a date, and she accepted. In her later years, Mrs. Schwarzkopf enjoyed telling how, "upon spotting him the following weekend in a parade, decked out in his uniform and riding a white horse, she pointed him out to one of her friends and said, 'That's the man I'm going to marry.'"[3]

Two girls, Ruth Ann and Sally, were born to the couple before Norman Schwarzkopf, Jr. During the fall of 1934, the Schwarzkopfs' first son arrived just as one of Colonel

Schwarzkopf's most famous investigations was starting to break—the Lindbergh baby kidnapping case. In March 1932, someone had kidnapped the infant son of famous American aviator Charles Lindbergh and his wife, Anne, who was the daughter of a U.S. ambassador. The Lindbergh baby was later found dead after Lindbergh paid a $50,000 ransom. For a year and a half, Colonel Schwarzkopf directed the investigation into the murder of the Lindberghs' son. In September 1934, a suspect was captured and arrested, an immigrant German carpenter named Bruno Richard Hauptmann. The case brought Colonel Schwarzkopf much media attention. The trial of the accused German resulted in his conviction in 1935 and his execution the next year.

Norman Schwarzkopf, Jr., remembers his youth as "a wonderful boyhood, filled with dogs, Christmases, birthdays, tree climbing and sled riding, and all kinds of friends."[4] The family lived in a modest home called the "Green House." Built in 1815, it was an ivy-shrouded stone structure on Main Street in Lawrenceville, New Jersey. Lawrenceville was about halfway between the state capital at Trenton and Princeton University.

Norman, Jr.'s younger years often involved boyhood mischief:

> Most days I rode my bike to school, down Main Street, left, up a ways, right, down that road, left, and up a hill. After class I'd link up with my friends Johnny Chivers, Billy Kraus, and Jimmy Wright. We'd spend nickels at the Jigger Shop, which was the town's most popular soda fountain, play cops and robbers, and smash empty Coca-Cola bottles on sewer grates. Near Johnny Chivers's house the trolley that ran from one end of Lawrenceville to the other crossed a little brook on a trestle about four feet high. One afternoon, after we got tired of defying death by walking on the rails, we snuck into Billy Kraus's father's farm and

pulled up some carrots and potatoes. Then we found an old tin can, filled it with brook water under the trestle, built a fire, and set the vegetables to cook. We felt very daring because this was just what hoboes did.[5]

Back home in the evenings, the family gathered around a radio in the living room to listen to popular radio serials, including *The Lone Ranger, The Shadow*, *The Green Hornet*, and a locally produced radio program called *Gang Busters*, which featured the elder Schwarzkopf himself.

After Schwarzkopf, Sr., stepped down from command of the state police, he took a job on the *Gang Busters* radio program, which reenacted important cases from the state's police files. Schwarzkopf, Sr., was the program's interviewer. Once the crime of the week was announced, the narrator set the stage for former Colonel Schwarzkopf: "We will now hear from the principal law enforcement officer who was involved in this heinous crime. He will be interviewed by Colonel H. Norman Schwarzkopf, former superintendent of the New Jersey State Police."[6] In later years, Schwarzkopf, Jr., described his father's performance on the radio as "absolutely fantastic."[7]

When he was six, Norman, Jr.'s family life changed dramatically. That year—1940—President Franklin Roosevelt called parts of the National Guard into active duty so they would be prepared if the United States had to enter World War II. Schwarzkopf, Sr., was in the National Guard, and his service kept him away from home on weekdays. Young Schwarzkopf remembered visiting his father at Camp Kilmer, a tent-dominated army community outside Princeton. On one such visit, in November 1941, his father showed him a copy of a book, *Mein Kampf*, written by the German dictator, Adolf Hitler. Although Schwarzkopf was only a small child, his father tried to explain to him that Hitler was "a bad man."[8]

Norman's father was in charge of the New Jersey state police during the investigation of one of the twentieth century's most sensational crimes — the Lindbergh baby kidnapping. Schwarzkopf, Sr., is seen here in a 1934 photograph, making a statement over the radio.

Just weeks later, Japanese planes carried out a surprise attack against the American naval and military base at Pearl Harbor, Hawaii. Suddenly, the United States was at war, and the household of the Schwarzkopfs changed. As a West Point graduate, Schwarzkopf, Sr., was chosen by Army Chief of Staff George Marshall to take an assignment overseas—not in Europe or Japan, where most of the war was being fought, but in the Middle Eastern nation of Iran.

By the time the United States entered World War II, the conflict had expanded to global proportions. American supplies, fuel, and other war goods were being shipped to the Soviets through the "Persian Corridor." So much war material was being diverted by Iranian raiders that the American government decided to send a West Point graduate who had both military and police experience to better train the Iranian police for wartime duties. That man was Colonel Norman

Schwarzkopf, Sr. It was 1942, and Norman, Jr., was not yet eight years old. When the announcement came that his father was leaving, Norman's mother showed her son where Iran and its capital, Tehran, were located, explaining that "Pop was about to travel to an exotic, magical, faraway place . . . where people wore long robes and carried knives in their belts and rode camels across the desert."[9]

Despite his mother's best intentions, Norman, Jr., still did not understand what was happening or how far away his father would be. The elder Schwarzkopf explained that he was going off to war and would be away for a long time. He handed young Schwarzkopf the army saber he had received when he graduated from West Point 25 years earlier, telling him, "I'm placing this sword in your keeping until I come back. Now son, I'm depending on you. The responsibility is yours."[10] The next morning, when young Norman woke up, his father was gone.

The war kept the family divided for several years. With Schwarzkopf, Sr., away, it was difficult for Mrs. Schwarzkopf to keep up with the household expenses, including the mortgage on their house. Norman's father sent letters from Iran to keep the family informed of his work and to say how much he missed them. The letters were exciting to Norman. He remembered that his father "had a set of colored pens and he'd illustrate the pages with intricate drawings of . . . marble palaces and mosques, bread riots, raids by wild mountain tribes, tedious diplomatic lunches. . . ."[11] There were packages, too, with all sorts of gifts for Mrs. Schwarzkopf and the children. For his tenth birthday, Norman received a 300-year-old Persian battle-ax. It was accompanied by a letter from his father:

> It really is something to have completed the first decade of your life, and to look back over the years and realize all the joy and pleasure that you have brought to Mommy and me.

. . . I am proud of you, my boy, and . . . [I] see a glorious future. Deep in Mommy's heart and my heart lie unspoken hopes and ambitions for you, an abiding love and understanding, and the knowledge that the success of our lives will be written in your deeds.[12]

Despite these optimistic words, all was not well in the Schwarzkopf home. Mrs. Schwarzkopf, facing both financial and emotional stress, had begun to drink heavily. Norman remembers his mother developing "a Jekyll-and-Hyde personality."[13] Sweet and sensitive one moment, she could become a mean, unbearable critic the next. Ruth Schwarzkopf made life miserable for her daughters, always nagging them and driving them to tears. As for young Norman, he had no defense but to "isolate myself as much as I could: get in there, have dinner, and disappear upstairs to my room."[14] He later wrote about his reaction to his mother's behavior:

I simply retreated, which Mom let me do because I was the youngest and her favorite. Deep inside me was a place where I would withdraw when things were unhappy at home. I discovered I could hide the painful feelings and still make friends and love dogs and help old ladies across the street and be a good guy. . . . I learned to be self-contained and independent. Maybe that was a gift my mother gave me.[15]

Through it all, Norman's father remained unaware of his wife's drinking problem.

Finally, by the spring of 1945, the war in Europe came to an end, as Allied forces advanced on the German capital of Berlin. The Schwarzkopf family began to hope that Norman, Sr., might come home soon. They soon received word, however, that his tour in Iran would not yet be ending. The Iranian leader, Shah Mohammed Reza Pahlavi, still needed American support in the face of a new challenge from the Communist Soviet Union. Norman Schwarzkopf, Sr., would have to stay at his post. He surprised his family, though, in June, when he was able to take a month's leave. Unfortunately, he, too, was surprised when he learned that his family was facing a serious crisis.

Scalping His Sisters' Dolls

As the youngest of the three Schwarzkopf children, Norman was often teased by his older sisters, who referred to him as "'Stupid,' as in 'Here's my stupid brother Norman' or 'Norman, you're so stupid.'"* The girls were not much older than Norman. Ruth Ann was the oldest by four years and Sally was just two and a half years ahead of him. Perhaps because of their closeness in age, Norman and Sally played together more often than Norman and Ruth Ann did. Sally liked to play outdoors while her older sister preferred to read and play the piano. When the three siblings did play together, a game might cast Ruth Ann as a princess, Sally as a general, and Norman as a lowly peasant.

There were days when Norman got the best of his sisters, however. On one rainy afternoon, the bored six-year-old could not think of anything to do. His mother remembered that she had recently taken him to a movie called *Geronimo*.

"Well, dear," she said, "Why don't you go upstairs and play Indian?"**

The idea instantly appealed to her imaginative son. He grabbed a hammer, ready to become the Indian leader he had seen in the movies. Norman bounded upstairs, raided his sisters' room, and used the hammer to "tomahawk" their dolls, punching "a hole in the forehead of each."*** Then he tried to scalp the toys.

When the girls came home to find their dolls "massacred," they showed their mother Norman's handiwork. When she asked why he had done it, he responded, "But you *told* me to play Geronimo!"****

* General H. Norman Schwarzkopf (with Peter Petre), *General H. Norman Schwarzkopf, the Autobiography: It Doesn't Take a Hero*. New York: Linda Grey, Bantam Books, 1992, p. 4.

** Jack Anderson and Dale Van Atta, *Stormin' Norman: An American Hero*. New York: Kensington Publishing, 1991, p. 16.

*** Ibid.

**** Schwarzkopf, p. 5.

Desperate for a way out of his depressing home life, Norman, Jr., asked if he could go to military school. His father had gone to military school, and Norman, Jr., claimed he was "tired of being in this house with nothing but girls. It's turning me into a sissy."[16] Three months later, Norman Schwarzkopf, Jr., enrolled in the Bordentown Military Academy as a sixth grader. He could not have been happier. Bordentown, New Jersey, was just south of Trenton. That meant he was not so far from his family that he felt isolated, but far enough away that, for those who lived there, the Schwarzkopf home became a very sad place.

Norman's father had worn a uniform as a boy, and now Norman was doing the same. Life at the academy required a lot of effort for eleven-year-old Schwarzkopf. The school was a serious place, "a big old white stone building with a parade ground out front and dormitories and playing fields behind."[17] He found the school more difficult than the elementary school he had attended in Princeton, but he was able to focus. There were fewer distractions, including "no pretty girls or radio shows or adventures with my buddies to distract me."[18]

That year, Norman, Jr., went through some significant developments. He sprouted up to nearly six feet (two meters) tall. His interest in sports increased, and he went out for soccer, as well as track-and-field events, including javelin throwing and tossing the shot put. All in all, military school life agreed with Schwarzkopf. He enjoyed the discipline and felt he was achieving his potential. By the end of the year, he was promoted to private first class, the highest rank possible for a sixth grader. For his class photograph, he posed with a stern look on his face. When his mother asked him why he had chosen such a stoic expression, he explained, "Someday, when I become a general, I want people to know that I'm serious."[19]

2

"Under My Father's Roof"

Having completed the sixth grade at the military academy in Bordentown, Norman did not look forward to returning home to witness his mother's drinking. He was relieved when his father, who had been absent in Iran for four years, suggested to Norman's mother that it might be best for the young man to come and live with his father. Mrs. Schwarzkopf asked Norman, Jr., what he thought of the idea. At first, the possibility of leaving home for the exotic world of Iran seemed unreal. When his mother repeated her question, however, he blurted out, "When do I leave?"[20]

It took a month to get a passport and permission to go from the Pentagon (U.S. military headquarters). Then, with everything in order and a suitcase packed, Norman, Jr., said good-bye as an army major in a white sedan pulled up to the family home to take him off to life in another world. It was August 22, 1946—Norman's twelfth birthday.

The trip took several days. Norman sat on an air force passenger plane that flew up the Atlantic coast to Canada, then east across the Atlantic to the Azores, and finally over the skies of recently war-torn Europe to Egypt. The final 1,000 miles (1,609 kilometers) crossed the deserts of the Middle East, and the temperature inside the cargo plane reached 100°F (38°C).

A pair of army aides met Norman at the airport in Tehran and drove him to his new home, a mountain villa outside the city. When they arrived, Norman's father came out to greet his son, but walked right past him, failing to recognize the tall young man who had grown so much after a year at military school. "I had to chase him down the steps and grab him," Norman wrote years later, "and we hugged. For the first time in four years I was under my father's roof."[21]

Norman's father had recently been promoted to brigadier general. In these postwar days, the United States and Iran were close allies, and Norman's father was at the center of that important international relationship. The world with which Norman, Jr., became familiar in Iran was like none he had ever dreamed of. It was an adult world, since there were no other children at the villa. His father shared a huge house with four other army officers and two of their wives. Rooms opened their French doors to swimming pools. An enormous dining room was complete with white marble floors and exquisite Persian carpets. Drinking water arrived in a large barrel brought in on a donkey cart from the American embassy and was stored in empty vodka bottles. Norman's room was "on the roof, where I could see south across the city

During World War II, Schwarzkopf, Sr., was sent to be an advisor to the shah of Iran. The Iranian capital of Tehran, seen here, was an exotic place that provided Schwarzkopf, Sr., with many interesting stories to tell his family back home.

and the desert that lay beyond." [22] The sights and sounds around him—long vistas of desert landscape, the quavering voices of the muezzins (criers) calling Muslims to prayer five times daily, the towering minarets that marked the locations of mosques—were constant reminders that he was living a dream that most boys his age could only read about in books.

Suddenly, the exotic pictures and illustrations his father had included in the many letters he sent home to his family during the war had come to life for Norman, Jr. Even so, most important for Norman was that he was with his father, whom he loved and respected very much. Reunited, they spent as much time together as Norman, Sr.'s work would allow. They hunted together and went horseback riding across the desert sands. One evening, his father told Norman they were going out. The two

Young Norman and the Crown Jewels of the Shah

During his first six months in Iran, there was always something new to dazzle young Norman's imagination, including a private showing of the shah's crown jewels. On one trip into Tehran, he was taken to the central bank of Iran, where he was directed to an underground vault. He stood in wonder as he gazed across a large room filled with "diamond-studded sashes and gem-encrusted golden swords. In the corners of the room were piles of emeralds and rubies. Piles!"

One treasure in particular caught the eye of the stunned American boy—a great globe at the center of the room. "It was solid gold," he later wrote. "All the oceans . . . were formed in emeralds, and all the countries—except Iran—in rubies. Iran was in diamonds." When he marveled aloud at the beauty of the globe, his interpreter responded matter-of-factly: "Oh, that's just something they made with leftover jewels."

Guided into a second, even larger vault, Norman's amazement was renewed as he looked at a chamber full of stacks of gold bricks. The Iranian guard in the gold vault spoke to him, and his translator told the young man, "He said to tell you that you can have all the gold you can carry out."*

Norman stepped forward and reached for a gold brick. Only then did he realize that every brick in the vault was too heavy for him even to lift, much less carry out of the vault. This gave the guards who protected the treasures of the shah a good laugh.

* General H. Norman Schwarzkopf (with Peter Petre), *General H. Norman Schwarzkopf, the Autobiography: It Doesn't Take a Hero*. New York: Linda Grey, Bantam Books, 1992, p. 33.

Schwarzkopfs rode into Tehran, where young Norman was surprised to learn they were to have dinner with a group of visiting tribesmen called the Baluchi. They reached the Baluchi tent encampment where "about twenty tribesmen in long robes and armed with rifles and knives talked to Pop and his interpreter while I waited nearby."[23] Young Norman found the tribesmen a bit intimidating as he sat down by his father for a meal of rice, fruit, raw vegetables, and a sheep roasted whole on a spit. During the meal, the tribesmen offered Norman a part of the sheep that they considered a delicacy—an eye. His father whispered to him that to refuse the food would be insulting to the tribesmen. Heeding his father's advice, Norman plopped the eyeball into a spoon and ate it whole. The tribesmen applauded, and his father was quite pleased. He later told him, "They were paying you a great tribute."[24]

For six months, the two Schwarzkopfs enjoyed their time together before the women of the family came to Iran to join them, bringing the family together at last. The villa outside Tehran was too small to accommodate everyone, so the Schwarzkopfs moved to a three-story private residence. It was, in fact, a small palace, filled with many servants. Young Norman's room was on the third floor, overlooking a "maze of houses, courtyards, other gardens, and alleys, all of which were hidden from the street."[25] It was just as exotic as the big villa where he and his father had lived, but things were soon very different.

His mother continued to drink, but she did so at home, out of the eyes of the public. She was often demanding, insisted on having her way, and still carped at the two girls, now 14 and 16 years old. As for Norman, much of the freedom he had enjoyed with his father was taken away because of restrictions placed on him by his mother. She did not let him call on servants. He could no longer attend his father's poker games and was not allowed to go to dinner parties. Norman was not happy with these changes. As he later wrote, "I felt that my mother and sisters had ruined my life. They were forcing me to go back to being a normal twelve-year-old boy."[26]

Norman, Jr., did not spend much time with his sisters, who were soon dating Iranian men—including the shah's half brother—despite their father's protests. Norman busied himself with hunting trips, tennis, and bicycling around the city with a friend named Michael. The two boys often rode out of the city to the Shemran hills on a rickety old Iranian bus with their bikes tossed up on top. They would then "coast all the way back down into Tehran, sharing the road with donkey carts and camel caravans."[27]

The dream life in the exotic world of postwar 1940s Iran did not last forever, though. By 1947, Schwarzkopf, Sr., was transferred to Geneva, Switzerland, and he took his family along. Norman was placed in a boarding school, Ecole Internationale (Ecolint). Here, Norman found "Switzerland's Alpine forests and blue lakes were an astonishing change from Iran's rocky deserts."[28]

The biggest problem Norman faced at the new school was language—nearly everyone spoke French, even the foreign students. After a few months, though, Norman, Jr., was getting comfortable and had a passing vocabulary.

At school, Norman's classmates were instantly impressed by his size. He had been tall for his age since sixth grade, and soon he was being sought out to play soccer, a major sport at the private school, because he "could kick the ball a mile and because I was so big."[29]

After a year at the school, Norman's father was transferred to a new assignment in Frankfurt, Germany.

In 1947, Norman and his family moved to Geneva, Switzerland, when
Schwarzkopf, Sr., was transferred. Norman thought the area, graced by
Lake Geneva (seen here) was picturesque.

There, Norman and his family lived in yet another
expansive house, one formerly occupied by wealthy Nazi
officials. The neighborhood where the Schwarzkopfs
lived was home to thousands of military families. There
was an American high school, attended by the children of
U.S. military personnel. Schwarzkopf, Jr., soon replaced
European soccer with another sport—American football.

Although Schwarzkopf had spent years away from
his life back in New Jersey, he soon immersed himself in

American culture. He searched catalogs for the most stylish jeans, shirts, and belts. He mingled with other American kids around Frankfurt and became popular. He balanced his after-school time between the army teen club and the PX (military base store) snack bar: "At the snack bar we'd sit for hours, drinking milkshakes, eating french fries, flirting with girls, and joking around. The teen club, across the park from my house, had a pool table and a jukebox."[30]

General Schwarzkopf's tenure in Frankfurt was short-lived. He was reassigned to duty in Heidelberg, 50 miles (81 kilometers) away, requiring another move for the family and another school—Heidelberg American High School—for Norman. He went out for football and was recruited. He played tackle and his team "beat all six American high school teams in Germany and won the European championship."[31] After a couple of years in Germany, his father was transferred to Italy, where he operated his office at the U.S. military mission in Rome. Norman, nearing age 16, attended yet another school, continued to participate in sports, served on the student council, and enjoyed the company of friends.

His experiences since leaving the United States back in 1946 made young Norman a well-rounded person, one who was familiar with several languages and knew his way around Europe. His youth was strewn with exotic details from the deserts of Iran to the streets of Rome, and he was a curious mixture of American, Indo-European, and everything in between.

Although these years offered unique opportunities to Norman, they were not entirely positive. His mother's drinking problem only worsened during this time. Because of her drinking, young Norman remained distant from his mother as a teenager. Her problem with alcohol embarrassed him and he felt powerless to do anything about it.

When he was a cadet at Valley Forge Military Academy, Schwarzkopf participated in several sports, among them tackle football. He is seen here in his football uniform.

His father did not help matters. He drank, too. Sometimes, his father even encouraged his mother to continue to drink. In his autobiography, Norman Schwarzkopf admitted that the family problem with alcohol left him with conflicting feelings about his father: "I loved him and admired him, but when he gave her alcohol, I hated him for it."[32]

By 1950, both father and son had agreed that the

military was to be Norman, Jr.'s future. That August, Norman boarded a troop transport ship bound for New York City. Norman had been accepted to Valley Forge Military Academy (VFM) on an athletic scholarship. The school was known as a preparatory institution for young men who intended to enter West Point after graduation. The VFM campus sat on 100 acres (41 hectares) in the hilly country outside Philadelphia. His old military school of younger days, Bordentown Academy, was only 40 miles (64 kilometers) away in neighboring New Jersey. Sixteen-year-old Norman saw the complete picture: "In a way, I'd come full circle."[33]

3

The Making of a Soldier

Having grown up in the shadow of military life, Valley Forge Military Academy was hardly a daunting place for Norman Schwarzkopf, Jr. He came to the campus as an imposing, six-foot two-inch, 200-pound, 16-year-old football player with much experience living in the world beyond the American East Coast.

The academy was run by General Milton H. Medenbach, who expected his cadets to live under a strict discipline that included daily inspection, challenging classwork, and an iron-clad dress code. From 6:00 A.M. to 9:30 P.M., Schwarzkopf's days were scheduled to the minute. On Sunday, all cadets were required to attend chapel service. Good grades were expected;

At 6 feet, 2 inches and 200 pounds, Schwarzkopf was a robust young man. His size helped make him an outstanding athlete in events such as shot-put throwing.

those who fell behind in their academic progress were placed on a "deficiency list."[34]

Yet Schwarzkopf excelled at VFM. He was caught violating the academy's rules on only one occasion, for throwing food at another cadet in the cafeteria. When the academy's Thanksgiving dinner included pasty, under-cooked pumpkin pie, the cadets, including Norman, protested by tossing their slices at one another. The transgression was placed in his permanent record.

For two years, Norman Schwarzkopf thrived under the tutelage and training he received at Valley Forge. He remained an excellent student, and it was at VFM that he was first administered an IQ test that revealed a score of 168. The importance of the score was made clear to him by a teacher who said, "Don't you realize you have the IQ of a genius!?"[35] When Norman graduated from Valley Forge in 1952, he was ranked at the head of his class of 150 cadets. He was valedictorian, an honor-winning debater, a star athlete in shot put and football, and the editor of the *Crossed Sabres*, the academy's yearbook.

Everything seemed to be pointing young Schwarzkopf toward West Point. Schwarzkopf shared his ambitions with a fellow member of his VFM troop: "I want to be a general. I'll be very disappointed if I don't make general."[36] His father, of course, was intent on his son's getting into West Point, as well. Entry into West Point was not a simple matter of hoping, however. It required perseverance on the part of both father and son.

That spring, as he graduated from Valley Forge, Norman was uncertain of his future. Appointments to West Point would not be made until the following month. Following graduation, he sat at home and anxiously waited. Then, on June 26, a telegram arrived:

ENTITLED ADMISSION WEST POINT AS COMPETITOR HONOR MILITARY SCHOOL STOP REPORT SUPERINTENDENT WEST POINT NEW YORK BEFORE ELEVEN OCLOCK AM DAYLIGHT SAVING TIME ONE JULY FOR ADMISSION AS CADET

Seventeen-year-old Norman Schwarzkopf had five days to prepare for his new life at the U.S. Military Academy at West Point. He proudly showed the letter to his father and mother, who cried. One of the first things he did was go to the local barber to get a crewcut.

When Schwarzkopf arrived at West Point, entering through the granite main gate of the old military institution, he brought little along but "a razor, a toothbrush, [and] a three-hundred-dollar check to cover toiletries and other essentials during the next four years."[37] He had

The Trials of a Boy Named Herbert

When Norman was born, his parents named him after his father, H. Norman Schwarzkopf, Sr. He grew up answering to the name Norman, and the "H" was avoided altogether. "Herbert" was a name both he and his father despised. However, at Valley Forge Military Academy, the dreaded "H" name caught up with him.

When students questioned Schwarzkopf about his first name, he told them it was only an initial, that the "H" did not stand for anything. Dissatisfied, the boys made up a name to go along with the "H," one that Norman hated as much as Herbert: Hugo. Schwarzkopf let the teasing get the best of him. During Christmas break of his sophomore year at Valley Forge, Norman asked his parents to go to Trenton, the New Jersey state capital, to access his birth certificate and legally change his name by discarding the "Herbert" and making the initial "H" officially part of his name.

That is exactly what Schwarzkopf, Sr., did. Although the original birth certificate showed "Herbert Norman Schwarzkopf, Jr.," the record was altered on January 2, 1952, to read "H. Norman Schwarzkopf." In making the change, the "Jr." was also eliminated.

All Norman's angst over his name did not end with the simple holiday trip to Trenton public records, however. Schwarzkopf's classmates got the last laugh in the senior yearbook at the academy. Members of the yearbook staff put a caption underneath his class picture that infuriated him once again: "Nickname: Hugo."

barely arrived when he began to receive instructions, orders barked at him by senior classmen "assigned to whip the new plebes [freshmen] into shape."[38]

As a plebe, Schwarzkopf faced the usual barrage of criticism, yelling, and humiliation that is dished out to every new student at West Point. Because his father was well known in the military, he was teased about him constantly. Some cadets knew about his father's old radio program, *Gang Busters*. They repeatedly ordered Norman to mimic the opening sequence to the crime drama: "Schwarzkopf! Give the *Gang Busters* poop!" Norman would then begin "stomping his feet, mimicking the rat-a-tat of a machine gun and then the wail of sirens."[39]

Being away from home was not a major problem for Schwarzkopf, since he had been at private schools for years. He understood how military life worked, was clear on the purposes of command and taking orders, and he understood his place as a plebe. He became very involved in extracurricular activities such as "[singing] in, and later [conducting] the choir; he wrestled, boxed, lifted weights, and played tennis, football, and soccer. In sports, as in his academic subjects, he was good but never the best in his class."[40] He was also a member of the German club.

By this time, he had become a tall, barrel-chested young man. Schwarzkopf struggled with his weight, though. It was part of his life at West Point that he never managed to bring under control. It kept him from excelling at sports in the same way he did at academics and other activities. It was difficult for him to do even three pull-ups.

The record Schwarzkopf accumulated at West Point was exemplary. He studied hard and found many of his classes worthwhile. One subject that fascinated Norman was the study of war, military leadership, and battle

Schwarzkopf excelled at West Point, not only in academics but in extracurricular activities. He even sang in the academy's choir.

tactics. It became his all-consuming interest. He was constantly reading histories of the great generals from America, Europe, and the ancient world. Two American generals held his keen interest. One was General George Patton, whose 3rd army had slugged its way across France and Germany during World War II. The other was General William Tecumseh Sherman, the hard-fighting

Union commander who took part in Civil War battles from Shiloh to Chattanooga. As for ancient commanders, he became well versed in the military exploits of the Carthaginian challenger to the Roman Republic, Hannibal. Greatest in Norman's mind, though, was Alexander the Great, conqueror of the ancient world from Macedon (on the Balkan Peninsula) to the Indus River Valley in southern Asia. Norman's experiences in Iran gave him a clear picture of Alexander's exploits in establishing a Hellenistic (Greek cultural) world, which he briefly dominated:

> In Iran, he had read about Alexander's formidable march through Persia [what is now Iran] in the fourth century B.C., conquering one city after another— Babylon, then Persepolis, then all of the Persian Empire. Since [he] had seen the terrain as a young boy, all this was vivid to him. And having witnessed his father playing a role in events of historic importance, he dreamed of doing great things himself. The Persian ax he had been given as a ten-year-old boy was not intended as a gift to a young man who would be satisfied with mediocrity.[41]

During his senior year, Norman Schwarzkopf achieved the cadet rank of captain, a significant achievement, but not the highest rank. Still, his new rank allowed him to hold command for the first time in his life. It was a responsibility that he took seriously. He was not overly abusive with his orders and hazing, and he even ordered his fellow cadets to back off when he thought their harassment of young cadets was nothing more than mindless abuse.

As his tenure at West Point drew to a close, Schwarzkopf faced a tough decision. Attendance at West

Point assumed that a cadet intended to go into military service as an officer for at least three years of active duty. Graduating seniors were encouraged to choose a branch of military service, such as artillery, armor, infantry, and engineering, among others. Armor and artillery were usually the most popular. Schwarzkopf, however, was not interested in either. He was prepared to put down his first choice as infantry.

For an excellent student such as Norman, one who was slated to graduate near the top of his class, the selection was extraordinary. Finishing 42nd out of 485 in the graduating class of 1956, he could have picked any branch and been assured of getting in. The infantry was what he wanted, though. His studies had convinced him that the real backbone of an army lay in its infantry. In fact, Schwarzkopf became so certain of the value of going into the infantry that he talked several of his friends into doing the same.

Graduation came on June 5, 1956. The graduation exercises capped a full week of "parades, speeches, ceremonies, concerts, and dinners" and also included "dozens of marriages in a cadet chapel."[42] Norman received his commission as a second lieutenant, graduating in the top 10 percent of his class. Schwarzkopf, Sr., hugged his son that day, shed a few tears, and shared the experience of seeing a dream come true for Norman, Jr. The new second lieutenant remembered in his autobiography years later, "more than any other day of my life, I felt like a good son."[43]

West Point had recreated Norman Schwarzkopf, Jr., in ways he did not then understand completely. Despite having grown up in a military world, it was his experience at West Point that gave him a clear vision of his own values. The academy motto—"Duty, Honor, Country"— had had no personal meaning for him before he entered

Schwarzkopf graduated from West Point with the class of 1956. His high academic standing and exemplary performance ensured that he would be able to secure a desirable position in the army.

as a first-year plebe. That changed dramatically during the four years he spent at West Point:

> I loved my country, of course, and I knew how to tell right
> from wrong, but my conscience was still largely unformed.
> By the time I left, those values had become my fixed
> stars. . . . The Army, with its emphasis on rank and medals
> and efficiency reports, is the easiest institution in the world
> in which to get consumed with ambition. Some officers

spend all their time currying favor and worrying about the next promotion—a miserable way to live. But West Point saved me from that by instilling the ideal of service above self—to do my duty for my country regardless of what personal gain it brought, and even if it brought no gain at all. It gave me far more than a military career—it gave me a calling.[44]

Within the ten years following his graduation in 1956, Second Lieutenant H. Norman Schwarzkopf would discover just how far that calling would take him in his pursuit of duty, honor, and country.

Youth Lost in Vietnam

Although newly graduated Second Lieutenant H. Norman Schwarzkopf chose the infantry as his branch of the service, he also selected a highly specialized unit of infantry in which to serve—the airborne infantry. Following graduation, he was sent to Fort Benning, Georgia, to attend airborne school where, along with specialized training, he learned how to parachute "fully armed and combat ready, from an airplane."[45] The next spring, he graduated once again and was assigned as a platoon leader with Company E, 2nd airborne battle group, 187th infantry regiment of the 101st airborne division. His new military home was Fort Campbell, Kentucky.

For two years, Schwarzkopf remained at Fort Campbell,

After leaving West Point, Schwarzkopf went to Fort Benning, Georgia, to take part in airborne training, like the students in this photograph. This student is going through a basic drill in which he jumps from a tower into a pile of sawdust.

although he was disappointed in what he saw while stationed there. As he later wrote, "I had an alcoholic commander and an executive officer who was a coward. I saw terrible things going on around me and I said, 'Who needs it?' When my three years are up, I'm getting out!"[46] Schwarzkopf explained, "West Point had filled my head with unrealistic expectations."[47]

While serving at Fort Campbell, Schwarzkopf was distracted by his father's declining health. Having smoked all his adult life, Norman Schwarzkopf, Sr., developed lung cancer. A stubborn man, he continued to chain-smoke even as his cancer was spreading. It appeared that nothing could make him "stop smoking his Kents."[48] On November 25, 1958, Schwarzkopf, Sr., died, a day before his son arrived home from Fort Campbell. Two days later, the funeral was held in West Orange, New Jersey.

As he watched the calendar turn to 1959, Schwarzkopf was downhearted by the death of his father, whom he had admired and loved very much. Uncertain of his future plans, he was deeply influenced by a conversation he had had with his new commanding officer, Major Tom Whelan, during the previous summer. When Schwarzkopf shared his disillusionment about the army with the major, Whelan told him: "There are two ways to approach it. Number one is to get out; number two is to stick around and someday, when you have more rank, fix the problems. But don't forget, if you get out, *the bad guys win*."[49] For the time being, Schwarzkopf decided to stay in uniform.

By the summer of 1959, he was assigned a new post, one he was somewhat familiar with already—Berlin, where his father had served a few years earlier. Taking up his duties as a platoon leader in Berlin, Schwarzkopf saw more of the military than he had been trained for at West Point. Because Berlin was considered part of the hot zone of Europe, there were constant drills, many field training exercises, and a command chain made up of tough, professional officers. Here, Schwarzkopf thrived, becoming an aide-de-camp to Brigadier General Charles Johnson. Within the Berlin command, 26-year-old Schwarzkopf was getting noticed by his superiors. He was also catching the eye of several young women in the American community in Berlin. One officer's high-school-age daughter noted: "We were all interested in whom he was dating, always watchful of the girls he was seeing—all these beautiful, sophisticated older women."[50]

In August 1961, Schwarzkopf returned to the United States, having been promoted to captain. Although he was sent to Fort Benning, Georgia, again, this time he went into a yearlong study called the Infantry Officers' Advanced Course. Any doubts he had once had about a career in the military had drifted away by this time. Schwarzkopf was an upwardly mobile young man and an eligible bachelor. The specialized training at Benning would qualify him as a master parachutist. His performance in the officers' training program earned him an invitation to teach for West Point's department of civil and mechanical engineering. However, he would have to earn a master's degree first, which he received from the University of Southern California in Los Angeles. The two-year program's rigors suited Schwarzkopf's academic mind, as he immersed himself in "studying missile mechanics and aerospace engineering."[51] He completed his degree in the summer of 1964. A three-year teaching appointment to West Point now awaited Captain Schwarzkopf, who would soon celebrate his thirtieth birthday.

Although teaching at West Point proved highly rewarding to Schwarzkopf, he was soon facing new distractions from a developing U.S. military involvement in Southeast Asia. By 1964, the American role in South Vietnam was shifting from one of providing military aid and training through noncombat advisors to one of deploying ground combat troops in the struggle against North Vietnam. That year, the campus of West Point was alive with talk about the expanding conflict in Vietnam. The academy even erected a "mock Viet Cong [VC] Village to train and orient the cadets toward that kind of fighting. It was a village of bamboo huts with straw roofs and defense positions along the trails approaching the village. Even the ambush sites were exactly like those of the Viet Cong [Communist troops in South Vietnam that worked to overturn the South Vietnamese government]."[52] For Schwarzkopf, the Vietnam War was both a calling and an opportunity, just as World War II had been for his father.

Schwarzkopf, however, had promised to teach at West Point for three years after his graduate school training, and he was still in his first year as an instructor. When he volunteered for active duty in Southeast Asia, he had to agree to come back after his tour in Vietnam and complete his teaching assignment. Schwarzkopf readily agreed. By June 1965, Schwarzkopf was on a military air command flight bound for the hot war of Vietnam.

American support for the South Vietnamese was in the midst of dramatic change when Schwarzkopf arrived. American military personnel in the country numbered between 75,000 and 80,000 that June, but another 50,000 arrived by August. Schwarzkopf's role in Vietnam that summer was not as a combat soldier but as an advisor to the Vietnamese airborne division, one of a handful of elite units of South Vietnamese troops. When he arrived, he found his work cut out for him. He was assigned as a "field advisor." As the name implies, field advisors did their work in the field, where they moved with South Vietnamese troops, informing them technically about combat and how to fight, but not engaging in armed conflict themselves. These officers were expected to "blend in with their Vietnamese counterparts so that they would not be singled out for attack in firefights."[53] Schwarzkopf, who, at six feet three inches, towered over the heads of most of his smaller Vietnamese allies, could hardly be expected to keep a low profile in the field.

While in Vietnam, Schwarzkopf, who was promoted to major soon after his arrival in country, saw several incidents of combat. He wrote in his autobiography, "I'd gone to Vietnam for God, country, and mom's apple pie. But by September I was fighting for the freedom of my South Vietnamese companions and friends."[54] One of his first actions was to help relieve 400 South Vietnamese troops who were surrounded by 3,000 North Vietnamese forces at Duc Co. The siege at Duc Co lasted several months. The defenders were dropped supplies and ammunition by air. Finally, about 1,000 South Vietnamese parachutists, as well as several American personnel, including Schwarzkopf, were dropped over Duc Co in support of their besieged comrades. When he and his men fell under attack, the

At first, the United States was technically not a combatant in the Vietnam War. American servicemen, however, were sent to serve as military advisors to the South Vietnamese. Schwarzkopf was one of those advisors. He is seen here (at front right) leading Vietnamese troops in August 1965.

young major ran "through enemy fire to get several wounded paratroopers back into the relative safety of the camp."[55] When the siege of Duc Co was finally broken that August, Schwarzkopf received a Silver Star for his bravery in rescuing the wounded from the field of battle.

Other medals soon followed, as Schwarzkopf continued to enter fights in support of his South Vietnamese troops.

Six months later, after engaging in a skirmish in which he exposed himself constantly to enemy fire, he again received the Silver Star. In that February battle, he was wounded four times, yet he insisted that his fellow wounded soldiers be treated before he received medical attention himself. He later received a Bronze Star for loading wounded soldiers onto a helicopter during a field engagement. During his first year in Vietnam, Schwarzkopf saw a relentless string of field fights. "We fought almost every day of every month for thirteen months," he remembered later. "I really thought we had done something good, just like George Washington. I had gone and fought for freedom."[56] He recalled the hectic, violent year of combat as "one of the best years of my life."[57]

After his year-long tour of duty, Schwarzkopf returned to the United States content with his service in Vietnam yet bewildered by the experience. When he first left home, he had still been the carefree bachelor in uniform. Now, he was more mature and more serious-minded, someone who had "lost his youth in Vietnam...."[58] Now in his early thirties, he was in search of a new direction.

As he had promised, he returned to West Point and began to teach again. He resumed dating a variety of women just as he had before leaving for Vietnam, but soon he zeroed in on one, Brenda Holsinger, an outgoing 27-year-old flight attendant, whom he met after a football game at West Point. That meeting led to a date the following week. After just two weeks of seeing one another, Schwarzkopf and Brenda were engaged.

Brenda was a Southern girl who was living in New York City at the time. The only child of Jesse and Elsie Holsinger of Timberville, Virginia, she had been raised on "an apple and chicken farm."[59] To Schwarzkopf, she was different from any girl he had ever known. Though she came from a small town, she had made her way in the sophisticated world of New York City. On July 6, 1968, they were married in the chapel at West Point, with Schwarzkopf wearing his white dress uniform.

After honeymooning in Jamaica, the newly married couple moved to Fort Leavenworth, Kansas, to Schwarzkopf's new command. Schwarzkopf had been chosen to attend the army's Command and General Staff College at Leavenworth, a prestigious appointment offered only to one of every three qualified officers. He was still on a fast track for advancement, having already achieved the rank of lieutenant colonel, which put him in front of nearly every one of his classmates from West Point.

One advantage Norman brought to his marriage was his own observations of his parents' sometimes difficult relationship and the strains of military life. He took extra care explaining to his new bride what problems they might face to help prepare her for the curves life might throw at the two of them. Although she was ready to face challenges, she could not know that over the next 20 years, she would have to move 16 times. She could not even know that her husband would accept a second tour of duty in Vietnam before the couple reached their first anniversary.

In July 1969, Schwarzkopf returned to Vietnam. In some respects, when he arrived in the country, it was as if he were entering a completely different war. The number of U.S. troops had ballooned to more than 500,000 and many of the soldiers there seemed to have lost much of their purpose and drive. Many were extremely young—19 and 20 years old—and a significant number had been drafted, sent to a war that they were not interested in fighting, and one that many Americans, including those in service in South Vietnam, considered unwinnable.

Schwarzkopf's reintroduction into Vietnam stirred deep feelings of anger and frustration in him. He had been sent to Vietnam to command a battalion in the 9th infantry division, stationed in the Mekong Delta, just south of Saigon. Once he arrived in Saigon, though, his assignment was changed. He was ordered instead to take a desk job at U.S. army Vietnam headquarters. It was a post he despised: "It was a cesspool. . . . You saw the worst there; the commander was living in luxury and his focus was on things like the re-enlistment rate."[60]

By November, he received the field command he had come to Vietnam to lead, assigned to the 1st battalion of the 6th infantry in the 198th brigade of the Americal division. That same month, he met Brenda for a weeklong leave in Hong Kong, and the two "had a honeymoon all over again—dining, dancing, going on harbor cruises, buying clothes for each other. . . ."[61]

On his return to Vietnam, Schwarzkopf took up his command, and was soon disappointed with his assignment. As he approached the base at Chu Lai by helicopter for the first time, the new commander thought it looked like "a damn gypsy camp. Nothing was camouflaged . . . and most of the men were up and moving around instead of resting for night operations."[62] Entering the camp, he came face to face with a military operation out of his worst nightmares:

> The guy who guided us in to land wore a pair of bright red shorts, flip-flops, and a yellow bandanna around his head, and had a three-day growth of beard. I jumped off and walked over to a lieutenant standing nearby—he had no helmet and no weapon, even though this was supposedly enemy territory. He did salute.
>
> "Lieutenant, where the hell's your weapon?"
>
> "Sir, it's over there, near my hammock."
>
> "Are you the company commander?"
>
> "No, sir. That's him, in front of the helicopter."
>
> The guy in the red shorts. I motioned him over and ordered him to put on his uniform and get his weapon.[63]

After a quick tour of the base, witnessing the lack of security and discipline, Schwarzkopf boiled over with anger and gave the captain a dressing down he was likely never to forget:

> Things are going to start changing around here, Captain, right now. *Right now.* My inclination is to relieve you of your command, but I can't do that because apparently this is the way you've been allowed to operate. But I'm telling you: you know what to do and it had better happen. First, when you stop someplace, you will put out security, and I mean *good* security. Second, I want every portable [transistor] radio out of the field. Third, I want every weapon in this outfit cleaned, and I'd better never come in again and find anybody without a weapon. Ever! . . . Fourth, I want every man, starting with you, shaved, cleaned up, and in proper uniform. With a helmet! [64]

It was the beginning of many changes for the men based at Chu Lai. Schwarzkopf wasted little time trying to put his mark on the men under his command. The new lieutenant colonel ordered his men to wear their helmets and flak vests when they were outside the firebase. He instituted new training programs and activities, as well as a tighter security system. In Schwarzkopf's view, the soldiers were falling victim to unpreparedness, not the enemy. Three out of every four deaths among the men of the 1st battalion of the 6th infantry were caused by booby traps and concealed explosives.

By the end of the year, Lieutenant Colonel Schwarzkopf's battalion was back in full military mode. Missions became more successful, and the casualty rate fell. Patrols pushed the Vietcong back, including the enemy's rocket attacks. When, in early January, Schwarzkopf's men tracked down and killed a Vietcong rocketeer, no more

Death by Friendly Fire

During his months in command, an incident occurred that reached the eyes of the media and the American public, one that placed Schwarzkopf in an uncomfortable position. When two of his men were accidentally killed by American artillery fire, a barrage of negative publicity followed. Such accidental deaths sometimes occur during large-scale military action. They are officially described as deaths "by friendly fire." They generally happen not because of poor judgment or incompetence, but as part of military combat. In this case, however, the parents of one of the young men killed, a sergeant named Michael Mullen, began to ask questions about their son's death. When they met resistance from the army, they became frustrated. They eventually "focused their anger on Schwarzkopf, blaming him for their son's death and accusing him of covering up the facts afterward."[*]

The story of the death of Sergeant Mullen became the subject of a book, *Friendly Fire*, published in 1976, after the Vietnam War was over. The book's author, C.D.B. Bryan, a writer for *The New Yorker* magazine, interviewed Schwarzkopf for the book, asking him about the details of the attack by friendly fire and his role in the aftermath of the tragedy. Bryan's view was that the incident was tragic, but that Schwarzkopf was not responsible for it. Bryan's book treated Schwarzkopf kindly, presenting him as "an honest and compassionate commanding officer."[**]

In his autobiography, Schwarzkopf presented a candid analysis of the Mullen story, admitting that the Pentagon had dealt poorly with the Mullens in the face of their personal tragedy. Schwarzkopf himself met with them and explained the details of their son's death. An artillery round, intended to strike a target beyond an American-held jungle trail, had struck a tree and exploded over the heads of some troops, killing Mullen and another soldier. Summing up the tragedy, Schwarzkopf noted: "To me the death of Michael Mullen was not just one tragedy but two: the needless death of a young man, and the bitterness that was consuming his parents."[***]

[*] Rebecca Stefoff, *Norman Schwarzkopf.* Broomall, PA: Chelsea House Publishers, 1992, p. 59.

[**] Ibid., p. 66.

[***] General H. Norman Schwarzkopf (with Peter Petre), *General H. Norman Schwarzkopf, the Autobiography: It Doesn't Take a Hero.* New York: Linda Grey, Bantam Books, 1992, p. 185.

rockets followed for another month. Some of the best news Schwarzkopf received during this period was a "captured enemy report that warned Vietcong units to stay away from LZ [landing zone] Bayonet [Schwarzkopf's firebase]. The report said a strong new American battalion had moved in." [65]

Toward the end of Schwarzkopf's tour of duty, a harrowing incident took place. On May 28, 1970, Schwarzkopf's men were searching for enemy positions along the Batangan Peninsula, a jungle and rice-paddy-covered region south of Chu Lai. Their lieutenant colonel was shadowing their movements from a helicopter overhead.

Then, a call came in over the radio. A group of soldiers—Bravo Company—had accidentally walked into a minefield and detonated the hidden explosives. Two men were wounded. Schwarzkopf ordered his helicopter pilot to fly to the site. What he found was a horrific scene of soldiers immobilized with fear. The soldiers of Bravo Company stood motionless on the minefield, afraid to move, to take even a single step that might detonate yet another hidden charge. Immediately, Schwarzkopf took charge of the situation.

He tried to calm the men in the field, and instructed them to back out of the minefield. In the process, a private stepped on another mine. The blast sent him skyward and he landed with a broken leg.

With a bleeding casualty in the midst of a minefield, Schwarzkopf found himself making a momentous decision, the kind commanders must make quickly. Out of the helicopter, he began to move into the minefield to rescue the frightened, wounded private. Slowly, step by step, Schwarzkopf moved toward the soldier, his breath short and sweat streaming down his face. After several agonizing minutes, he reached the wounded man, examined the

His heroic actions in leading troops out of a dangerous minefield helped Schwarzkopf earn his third Silver Star medal, seen here.

break, and called for a splint to bind up the leg. Just as another soldier grabbed a knife and moved toward a tree to hack off branches for the needed splint, he stepped on another mine. Three soldiers were killed in the explosion. At that moment, the medevac (medical evacuation) team arrived and began to treat the wounded. The injured private was removed from the deadly minefield. Schwarz-kopf emerged from the minefield a hero and Silver Star recipient.

By the time Schwarzkopf left Vietnam at the end of his second tour of duty in June 1970, he had received three Silver Stars, two Oak Leaf clusters, two Purple Hearts, three Bronze Stars, and several other medals. As he prepared to leave, he boarded a chopper and flew out to pay a final call on each of his units in the field. He told them, "My time is up. I am going back to the United States. I tried my best. I tried to save as many lives as possible."[66]

5

Recovery

Although Norman Schwarzkopf always remembered his first tour of duty in Vietnam (1965–1966) as one of the best years of his life, he found his second tour extremely disappointing. It was not that he was dissatisfied with his performance as a commander. He had pushed for and received a frontline combat command and had reorganized his men to perform better in the field and avoid being killed because of haphazard conditions. What most disturbed him was how the war had changed and how it was affecting his fellow citizens back home. "I hate what Vietnam has done to our country!" he noted in an interview after his return to the United States. "I hate what Vietnam has done to our Army." [67]

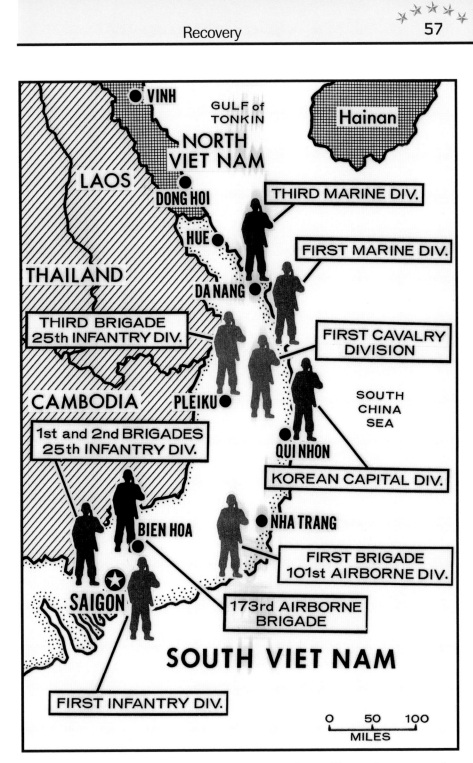

U.S. and South Vietnamese troops were spread out all over the country in the struggle to drive the Communist North Vietnamese out of the south.

To many people in the United States, including his own sister, Schwarzkopf was no hero at all. This new development nearly drove Schwarzkopf out of military service altogether. As one historian explained:

> For many professional soldiers of Schwarzkopf's generation, the situation was profoundly disorienting. They had grown into manhood during the 1950s, at a time when America's ability to grow richer, do good, and influence the world had never seemed stronger. They had an almost naïve belief in American power: first General [Dwight David] Eisenhower had freed Europe from Hitler, and then, between 1952 and 1960, President Eisenhower had made the country richer than ever. Their view that America should serve as the model for the free world was largely unquestioning. Their decision to go to Vietnam stemmed from the same absolute conviction: the South Vietnamese people should live in freedom and democracy and be rid of the menace of Communism. Yet here before their eyes was the abject result of what they saw as an essentially noble effort: a discredited military—undisciplined, divided, hesitant, derided.[68]

What made it worse for Schwarzkopf was that he had chosen the military as his lifelong career. He emerged from his Vietnam experiences disillusioned, and he began to give serious thought to leaving the army.

Schwarzkopf gave special credit to his wife, Brenda, for helping him through the professional crisis he went through after his tour in Vietnam. "I hate to think what my life would have been like if I hadn't had Brenda to come back to after Vietnam," he wrote.[69] Through the summer of 1970, when she was in the third trimester of her first pregnancy, Schwarzkopf relied on Brenda for moral support. In late August, the two celebrated Schwarzkopf's thirty-sixth birthday by going to his sister Sally's cabin outside Bethesda, Maryland. There, "Norman talked about the war and his ambivalent feelings," trying to work out his thoughts about Vietnam while surrounded by his family.[70] Returning to a more normal life with his wife helped distract him from his inner struggle. A month after his return from Vietnam, on August 23, Brenda gave birth to their first child, a daughter named Cynthia.

Despite the pleasure he took in his family, Schwarzkopf's personal demons regarding Vietnam continued to haunt him. He could not seem to forget the war. Because he remained in the military and held a post in the Pentagon with the officer personnel directorate of the infantry branch, the war was never far from his mind. Fortunately, Schwarzkopf tried to talk through his feelings about his Vietnam experiences. He spoke often with Brenda and his sister Sally, who was opposed to the war. He spent time talking to friends and colleagues, and even meeting with former classmates in the military. These talks were never discussions about the war itself, but about how the war had divided the country.

His experiences in Vietnam had exposed him to a military system that was certainly less than perfect. Everywhere in Vietnam, especially during his second tour, he had seen how "carelessness, negligence, lousy leadership, and self-serving officers and generals cost human lives."[71] He was angered by politicians and army officers alike who approached the war with more concern for their personal careers than for the soldiers in the field who risked their lives daily. He was sickened by officers in Vietnam who kept no council with their troops and remained out of sight, living a high life of self-indulgence. Schwarzkopf had always been a hands-on soldier, spending time close to his men, eating the same food they did, and putting himself in harm's way. As a result, even as he toyed with the idea of resigning his commission, Schwarzkopf became more determined to stick with it, if for no other reason than to be part of the solution. He wanted to work to fix the mistakes and heal the damage created by a military that sometimes destroyed its own from within. So Schwarzkopf decided to remain in the U.S. army and work to improve the character of the American military. His wife, Brenda, was supportive. With the war behind him, he and Brenda enjoyed a reasonably normal family life, and Brenda gave birth to their second child, another girl, who was named Jessica.

The early 1970s continued to witness Norman Schwarz-kopf's rise through the ranks. He attended the U.S. Army College in Carlisle, Pennsylvania, from August 1972 through June 1973. This was considered a requisite for advancement from the rank of lieutenant colonel or colonel. It was from each year's class of graduates that future generals were selected, a dream Schwarzkopf had fostered since his West Point days.

After this special training, he returned to Washington, D.C., to take a post at the Pentagon. He was assigned to the financial management office. It was another desk job that Schwarzkopf hated. Despite the army's experiences in Vietnam, the military was moving into a new era. After Vietnam, there would be no more draft. The army's future would be shaped instead by an all-volunteer force. This worried Schwarzkopf greatly. As unattractive as the military had become in America, he could not imagine what kind of recruits would be drawn to service. Meanwhile, just as the army was hoping to recruit the next generation of U.S. soldiers, it was also launching plans for a new period of American weaponry, including designs for Apache and Black Hawk helicopters, Patriot and Pershing missiles, and a new M-1 tank. At his desk in the Pentagon, it was Schwarzkopf's job to fit these costly weapons development programs in the army's annual budget.

Despite these significant opportunities to reshape the U.S. military, as well as his selection to the War College, the early 1970s were less than rewarding years for Schwarzkopf. He seemed aimless, a soldier between wars. Events in Vietnam did not help Schwarzkopf reconcile his own anguish. On January 27, 1973, the United States and North Vietnam reached a cease-fire agreement and American involvement in the war came to a close.

What Schwarzkopf always wanted was to be in command of a unit in the field. Desperate for such a command, he accepted the post of deputy commander of Fort Richardson's 172nd infantry brigade. The posting was one no other officer wanted—in Anchorage, Alaska. That fall, he packed up his family and headed north.

In his new command, Schwarzkopf tried to redefine his role as a U.S. military officer, turning Richardson into a personal experiment. Schwarzkopf commanded in Alaska as he had done in Vietnam. He did, however, loosen the reins in delegating tasks to his subordinates, showing them that he trusted their abilities and judgment to make rational field decisions. He was less harsh and volatile in the cooler climate of Alaska. He pushed his men hard, putting them through winter maneuvers that included lengthy foot marches and a simulated battle that lasted 11 days and included 4,000 troops. The refined humanity of his command led his men to give him a nickname—"the Bear."

The landscape around Fort Richardson seemed to be a tonic to Schwarzkopf. He loved the wildness of the landscape. He took Brenda and his two daughters on camping trips that included mountain hikes, fishing, and sleeping in the family camper. The rugged beauty of Alaska recharged the spiritual batteries of a soldier

Schwarzkopf had always wanted to lead his own unit. In 1973, his wish came true when he was given command of the 172nd infantry brigade, stationed at Fort Richardson, Alaska.

who had emerged from Vietnam with serious personal doubts:

> Moreover, when the troops were not on bivouac, he spent time outdoors on his own. Brenda would drop him off at the edge of a mountain trail and come back for him three days later. He would thus spend long periods by himself—

Despite the fact that his post in remote Alaska was one few other officers would have wanted, Schwarzkopf (right) was pleased with his command and set out to make his unit as efficient as possible. Although he demanded that his troops have discipline, he also won a reputation as a caring leader who did his best to help each individual soldier.

away from people and problems—alone except for the salmon, the trout, and a few real bears. It was a spiritual and physical exercise, one that even managed to rekindle his love for hunting. Up there, alone in the wilderness of Alaska, he was finally at peace.[72]

The following year, 1975, brought a series of changes in Schwarzkopf's life, including both personal victories and challenges. He became a full colonel. Although he and his sister Sally had grown apart, largely due to her earlier opposition to the war in Vietnam, Schwarzkopf was able not only to reconcile his personal feelings about the war, but also his relationship with his sister. On April 30, Schwarzkopf sat in front of a television set and watched as the city of Saigon, South Vietnam, fell under Communist control. The Vietnam War had resumed after the last American troops left the country two years earlier, and the South Vietnamese army had finally been overwhelmed. One of the last units still fighting against the onslaught of the North Vietnamese was Schwarzkopf's airborne force. He could only imagine the desperate circumstances the men were facing: "I knew that the airborne's cause was lost and that men who were my friends . . . were probably fighting to the death, at that moment."[73]

In October of the next year, Schwarzkopf's mother, Ruth, died. He did not get to see her, as he and his sister Ruth arrived the day after her death. The funeral brought the three Schwarzkopf children together for the first time in years. A swirl of feelings and strong emotions went through Schwarzkopf during those days. He recalled:

> I had loved my mother—in my own way I had managed to separate the woman she was from the alcoholic she became—and now I would never see her again. I grieved for the opportunity we'd lost. We could have been a close, loving family, but alcoholism had driven us apart; and while I'd realized years ago that the warmth I'd longed for would never be, her death put an end to that dream.[74]

That same month, Schwarzkopf received a new command, which required yet another move for him and his family. He was to lead the 1st brigade of the 9th infantry division at Fort Lewis, in Tacoma, Washington. At the same time, Brenda discovered that she was pregnant again. Schwarzkopf had long hoped for a son. That dream came true in the summer of 1977, when Brenda gave birth to a boy, whom Schwarzkopf named Christian, after his great-grandfather.

As for the 3,000 men under his charge at Fort Lewis,

Schwarzkopf pushed them hard. His stint at Fort Lewis lasted for two years and was followed by a reassignment to Hawaii as deputy director for plans, U.S. Pacific Command. Although he did not command soldiers at this desk job, he had to perform in a highly organized manner, serving diplomatically as a representative of the Pentagon with U.S. allies in the Pacific. He traveled to Korea and other Asian nations. He also honed valuable skills that better qualified him for further advancement in rank. On August 1, 1978, he received such a promotion, becoming a brigadier general.

In 1980, another transfer came in, this time to Mainz, West Germany, where he became assistant commander of the 8th infantry division (mechanized). The Mainz posting placed Schwarzkopf in command of an 11,000-man force. For two years, he worked to reshape the 8th infantry into the disciplined force he envisioned. As always, he was a hands-on commander, and one who was extremely accessible to his men. He even informed the wives of the servicemen in Mainz that he wanted to hear about their lives and any problems they thought he might be able to address. His open-door policy won him a reputation as a great promoter of "army-family support."[75] To Schwarzkopf, his command had to be "a well-run community for his troops because he believed, as he would often point out to his staff, that a happy soldier is a better soldier."[76]

During his two years in Germany, Schwarzkopf was able to explore his family's German roots. He made frequent connections with Germans in the Mainz community. He and his two daughters participated in a *Volksmarschverein*, a local walking club, taking ten-kilometer (six-mile) hikes on weekends along with hundreds of German families. It had been decades since Schwarzkopf lived in Germany when his father had been stationed there, and "as we tramped across the country-side and chatted with the Germans, I felt as if I'd picked up my connection where I'd left off in Berlin twenty years before."[77]

During his tour of duty in Germany, Schwarzkopf

Ham and Cheese Sandwiches, Anyone?

While in command of the army base at Mainz, Germany, Schwarzkopf worked hard to establish friendly relations with the local townspeople. On one occasion, when the general tried to mix diplomacy, hospitality, and profit-making, things did not go according to plan.

Because Schwarzkopf spoke German reasonably well, he was able to establish a working friendship with the mayor of Mainz, who informed the American commander in 1980 that Pope John Paul II was scheduled to visit the city in mid-November. The mayor requested the use of some of the facilities at the American military post.

Schwarzkopf agreed, but before signing off on any arrangement to host the pope's visit, the general had the Mainz mayor agree to allow the American base to have the concession rights. Since half a million people were expected to come for the pope's visit, the potential profits could amount to hundreds of thousands of dollars. Concessionaires were contracted to prepare gallons upon gallons of hot cider and hundreds of thousands of ham and cheese sandwiches. Schwarzkopf intended to sell the sandwiches for $1.50 each and use the profits from the food and drink sales to help defray the cost of providing special services to his troops and their families, including day care and other family programs.

Finally, the day of the pope's visit came and the Americans readied themselves for great crowds and profits. The event, however, did not work out as expected, as Schwarzkopf describes in his autobiography:

"It was a blowing, freezing, drizzling day, and the crowd numbered only three hundred thousand rather than the five hundred thousand we'd expected. . . . Thanks to the cold weather and unexpected small turnout, the [base] now owned one hundred thousand leftover ham-and-cheese sandwiches. . . ."[*]

* General H. Norman Schwarzkopf (with Peter Petre), *General H. Norman Schwarzkopf, the Autobiography: It Doesn't Take a Hero*. New York: Linda Grey, Bantam Books, 1992, p. 229.3

again advanced in rank, this time to major general. The promotion was a true honor. Only one out of every two one-star generals ever receives his or her second star, and the advancement signified the "highest rank in the Army decided upon by a promotion board that weighted all eligible candidates in open competition."[78] He received the coveted second star during a ceremony on July 1, 1982. The occasion included a speech that Schwarzkopf delivered with a voice that "started cracking and tears welled in his eyes."[79] Even as he accepted his great honor, he had already been informed of an impending transfer. He would soon be leaving the 8th mechanized infantry division.

Just a month later, Schwarzkopf took up new duties, once again, at the Pentagon. Although he continued to dislike shuffling papers, he realized that the U.S. army, in which he had been serving for more than 25 years, was changing. The armed services had emerged from the Vietnam War defeated and their morale was in shambles. The volunteer army program created after the war had achieved mixed reviews and limited success. Recruitment roles went unfilled and too many of those—two out of three—who signed up for military duty were placed in the army's "category four"—soldiers with low IQs of 60 to 80. By 1980, fewer than half of the soldiers in the army had graduated from high school.

When Ronald Reagan was elected president in November 1980, however, the military soon underwent some of the most important changes it had experienced since the Vietnam War. The new president "placed a heavy emphasis on defense . . . with weapons programs for America's might. As a result, the Army became more attractive. It commanded bigger budgets and a bigger share of attention."[80] The changes were clear to Schwarzkopf at his new Pentagon job as the director of

Several times throughout his long career, Schwarzkopf was assigned duties at the Pentagon (seen here). Although he preferred action in the field to the paperwork his Pentagon jobs required, he used his time at the nation's military headquarters to help reorganize the ailing U.S. armed forces.

the army's personnel department. Under the army's new recruiting slogan "Be All That You Can Be," the average recruit, by 1983, was a vast improvement over the immediate predecessors. By that year, 90 percent of those serving in the U.S. army were high school graduates.

After ten months at the Pentagon, yet another of General Schwarzkopf's lifelong dreams became a reality. In June 1983, he became a divisional commander, assigned to the 24th infantry division (mechanized), stationed at Fort Stewart, Georgia. It was an assignment that Schwarzkopf had always longed for. The 24th was one of the best-trained divisions in the army.

When Schwarzkopf arrived at the immense base, he found "every vehicle—every tank, supply truck, armored personnel carrier, and jeep—was painted in desert camouflage."[81] The 24th had been designated as the first armored division to be deployed in the event of U.S. involvement in a war in the Middle East. The 24th was one of a triad of divisions, including the 82nd airborne and the 101st air assault.

Just months after taking his command at Fort Stewart, Schwarzkopf received a telephone call after a Sunday afternoon of bass fishing. It was Major General Dick Graves, the director of operations at Forces Command, serving under General Richard E. Cavazos. Cavazos had been Schwarzkopf's commanding general five years earlier at Fort Lewis, Washington. He had since become the commanding general of the U.S. Army Forces Command in Atlanta.

Graves asked Schwarzkopf, "What have you got lined up for the next few weeks?"

Schwarzkopf was blunt: "What's this all about?"

"I need to know," said Graves. "You're being considered for a very important mission, and General Cavazos asked me to find out your plans."[82]

When Schwarzkopf finally hung up the phone, he was certain that he and his forces were going to be deployed to the Middle East. He soon discovered otherwise, however. He and the troops under his command were to be sent to the Caribbean island of Grenada.

6

"They're Not Going to Fight"

The island of Grenada was tiny, one-third as large as Fort Stewart's 285,000 acres (115,335 hectares). The island had been part of the British Empire until it gained its independence in 1974. For the next five years, the island was governed by Sir Eric Gairy, a right-wing autocrat whose government was one of "harsh repression, rampant corruption, and a flagrant misuse of the island's extremely moderate resources."[83] Despite being poorly led, however, Grenada was friendly to the United States.

Then, in 1979, a Socialist coup overthrew the corrupt Gairy. Thirty-four-year-old politician Maurice Bishop led the revolt and declared himself prime minister. During the intervening years, Bishop aligned his country more closely with

Communist-controlled Cuba. In 1982, Bishop paid a visit to Moscow and agreed to allow the building of a Soviet communications facility in his country, as well as a military airfield, even though Grenada itself had no air force. Despite his overtures toward the Soviets, by the summer of 1983, Bishop had begun to back away from Soviet support and was making attempts to renew relations with the United States. This move led to his removal by a pro-Soviet faction inside his political party. When Bishop was arrested and ousted from office, the U.S. government became alarmed that a Communist takeover of the island was coming. Another concern was the fact that Grenada had a private medical school where 400 American medical students were in residence. Their safety was an important concern.

With Bishop's arrest, General Cavazos received word from the Pentagon to begin organizing an invasion force to dispatch to Grenada. The command structure of the planned mission to Grenada quickly became complicated, since the invasion was to take place on a Caribbean island, which lay within the military's Atlantic command, a joint command of the army, navy, air force, and marines. As Cavazos planned the invasion, Bishop was killed by pro-Soviet Grenada forces whose leader, General Hudson Austin, established military rule. Two days later, the leaders of several Caribbean nations, including Barbados and Jamaica, appealed to the United States to intervene as soon as possible. By October 24, Schwarzkopf had been informed of the planned mission to Grenada. On paper, the invasion appeared to be a textbook operation:

> A Marine contingent was supposed to arrive by helicopter
> on the northern part of the island to gain control of Pearls
> Airport and then move south toward the capital of

The 1983 American invasion of Grenada was intended to put down a violent overthrow of the small island nation's democratic government. Here, U.S. troops raise the American flag at Point Salines Airport in Grenada during the military campaign.

St. George's. Simultaneously, the Rangers were to be parachuted to the southern tip to seize Point Salines airfield and then immediately move a few miles north to the True Blue campus, where the American students were. From there, they would then march north toward the capital to join the Marines.[84]

Although the plan seemed simple, Schwarzkopf had plenty of questions after his briefing. The Grenadian army included several thousand troops, but the general was assured they would not fight when they realized they were up against Americans. There were between 600 and 800 Cubans at the Point Salines airfield, who had military training, Schwarzkopf said. His military briefers again tried to put his mind at ease: "They're not going to fight."[85] Schwarzkopf's main role was to coordinate the invasion with the commander of the helicopter carrier *Guam*, Vice Admiral Joseph Metcalf III. This ship would serve as the primary invasion vessel.

The mission was code-named "Urgent Fury." Although Schwarzkopf was excited about the possibility of engaging his troops in a combat theater, any attack on the Caribbean island in question would constitute the first time American troops had "attacked an enemy in a foreign country"[86] since the Vietnam War. On the evening of October 24, Schwarzkopf stood on the deck of the aircraft carrier *Guam* and wondered what lay before him: "Are we getting involved in another Vietnam? Is this something the American people will or will not support?"[87]

In the predawn hours of Tuesday, October 25, 1983, American forces launched their attack on Grenada. Within 45 minutes of one another, 400 marines left the *Guam*, and 500 Rangers were flown in from an airfield in Barbados, bound for targets in Grenada. Although the Marines landed with little resistance, the Rangers encountered heavy artillery fire — resistance Schwarzkopf had been assured would not take place. Meanwhile, Schwarzkopf and Vice Admiral Metcalf monitored the invasion from the flag-plot room onboard the *Guam*, which was positioned just a mile from the Pearls Airport where the marines had been dispatched.

During the first two hours of the island operation, the marines captured Pearls Airport with little incident. At Point Salines, however, the Grenadians and Cubans who were supposed to have surrendered at first sight of the Americans put up a two-hour gun battle against the

Rangers. Schwarzkopf described the high level of resistance in his autobiography: "At first we got only fragmentary reports, but it was clear that this was no cakewalk. People were getting killed."[88]

By 8:30 A.M., the Rangers had secured their perimeter and moved on the medical school to help evacuate hundreds of American students at the site. Only then did the military, including Schwarzkopf, realize that the Point Salines campus was only one part of the school. An additional 224 American students were at a second school at Grand Anse, two miles (three kilometers) away, and that site was still in the hands of Cuban and Grenadian forces. Pentagon officials ordered in reinforcements that afternoon, including two battalions of the 82nd airborne division.

By then, Schwarzkopf and Metcalf were busy altering the original attack plan, resetting timetables, ordering attacks at new locations, and generally making up the battle as they went along. When a couple of dozen navy special forces, SEALs, became pinned down in the home of the island's governor-general by Grenadians and Cubans who arrived on armored amphibious vehicles, Schwarzkopf organized and ordered a landing of several hundred marines and five tanks on the evening of the first day of fighting.

That night, Vice Admiral Metcalf called a meeting of his commanders aboard the *Guam*. After watching Schwarzkopf in action that day, Metcalf placed the innovative general in the role of deputy commander of operations. At 3:00 A.M., as the second day of the conflict opened, Schwarzkopf ordered a newly improvised marine company into Grenada toward the governor-general's house, where they provided support for their fellow marines, who were besieged in the residence. Then, they rescued the governor-general and his wife. The problem of the American medical students at Grand

Although the planners of the operation did not expect opposition from the enemy forces on Grenada, when the American forces landed at Point Salines airfield (seen here), they faced a two-hour battle against the Grenadian and Cuban forces in control of the island.

Anse, however, still remained. Cuban and Grenadian forces were holding up the overland advance of the Rangers toward Grand Anse.

Schwarzkopf, though, had figured out a strategy to achieve that goal as well. By October 26, the *Guam* had sailed from just off the coast near the Pearls Airport to the south end of the island, within sight of the medical school that had become the new objective. Later in the morning, Schwarzkopf hit on an alternative solution:

> I stepped outside [on the deck of the *Guam*] for a moment of peace. Standing on the bridge, I looked straight across at the students' building, which was

fronted by a long stretch of white, sandy beach. Then I looked directly down onto the flight deck and focused on the dozens of Marine helicopters just sitting there. Why were we fixated on attacking over land? I went back inside, where Metcalf was talking with his staff . . . and brought him back out on the bridge. "Listen, that's where the enemy is, right over there. Look at that beach. It's a perfect landing zone! We've got all these helicopters here, and all those Rangers and Airborne troops down at Port Salines. Why not pick up the troops, fly in from the sea, and rescue the students?"

"Great!" Metcalf exclaimed. "Make it happen."[89]

Once the marine helicopters were made available, the rescue mission was set in motion within just a few hours. Six helicopters that carried armed marines and Rangers landed at Grand Anse. Less than half an hour after landing, all 224 American students had been evacuated with only two Rangers wounded. Again, Schwarzkopf's creative thinking had brought about another success for the invasion of Grenada.

By the end of the third day of fighting, Operation Urgent Fury had accomplished its mission in Grenada. Schwarzkopf considered it a success, since American forces had secured all their objectives, including the evacuation of the medical students. That fact alone convinced the general, who had questioned the mission and its purposes at first, that the operation was justified. After he "saw the rescued American medical students kiss the ground at a U.S. airport, he was 'one hundred percent sure we did the right thing in Grenada.'"[90]

Although the success of the mission never appeared to be in danger, the American military had made serious errors. The mission had taken too long and had resulted in the deaths of 19 American military personnel. There were

One of the main goals of the Grenada mission was to rescue a large number of American students who had been attending a university on the island. In this photograph, a soldier from the 82nd airborne unit poses with a group of grateful students in October 1983.

lingering questions about how fewer than 700 Cubans and several hundred Grenadian troops were able to impede the progress of American troops on the island for as long as they did, considering that, by the end of the third day of the invasion, American military personnel in Grenada included 900 marines, 500 Rangers, and more than 5,000 paratroopers of the 82nd airborne division.

After the fact, one of Schwarzkopf's primary concerns

about the mission was that he and his fellow commanders had gone into the invasion without complete and accurate intelligence data. From his experiences in Grenada, the general learned a valuable lesson: "Schwarzkopf saw that first-class, up-to-date intelligence reports were vital to a smooth-running operation."[91]

By November 3, Schwarzkopf was back in the United States. When his plane landed at Fort Stewart, he found

> a crowd of people waiting. Fifty or sixty people cheered and waved American flags as we taxied up. I could see Brenda, Cindy, Jessica, Christian . . . as well as the 24th Mech band. I was moved almost to tears. I'd come home from war twice before, but I'd never received a welcome. I hadn't expected one now, and it made me feel like a million dollars.[92]

Brenda and the children had also brought along the family dog, a black Labrador named Bear.

Back at Fort Stewart, Schwarzkopf continued to make policy changes designed to give support to his men, both professionally and personally, as well as their families. His motto was clear: His troops and their well-being came first. Sometimes the changes he made were simple, such as keeping the commissary open on Sundays so soldiers' families could shop on the base. A shuttle bus system was established to bring families to the base to use the PX, which generally offered household items cheaper than civilian stores. On August 3, 1984, Schwarzkopf initiated the first-ever Family Day at Fort Stewart, which gave soldiers the day off if they brought their families to the base for an open house. There were many special events, such as a prize raffle, a pie-eating contest, and games and rides.

Schwarzkopf even brought a Burger King franchise to Fort Stewart, one of the first on any American military base. The fast-food restaurant opened in April 1985, and proved extremely popular with the troops and their families. The deal was good for Fort Stewart. As Schwarzkopf arranged it, half of the restaurant's profits went to the base. Some of that money was used to build a swimming pool at the fort.

By the summer of 1985, Schwarzkopf's two-year tour

Have a Merry Schwarzkopf Christmas!

During his lengthy military career, Norman Schwarzkopf maintained a constant interest in making the U.S. military a better system. He looked for as many ways to boost the morale of his troops as he could, regardless of where he was stationed or even what the official policy of the military was on certain subjects. One such incident occurred during the Christmas season in 1983, after he returned from the mission to Grenada.

When he returned to his command at Fort Stewart and the 24th infantry division, he discovered that the Pentagon had sent down a directive banning Christmas lights on all military bases and posts, as well as at the homes of soldiers living on base property. Schwarzkopf, who believed the holiday was an important family occasion, chafed under the ruling. Although he understood that the army's rationale was to save money and support an energy conservation program, he decided that the fort would not cooperate. He allowed the men and women of the 24th mechanized to hang lights on the base and at their homes. Soon, General Cavazos, Schwarzkopf's direct superior officer, gave him a call, asking about the infraction of Pentagon rules.

"Oh, you found out about the Christmas lights," Schwarzkopf said.

Cavazos responded, "Yes, I have. . . ."

"Have you also found out about the personal check for four hundred dollars," asked Schwarzkopf, "that I made out to the U.S. government to pay for the electricity?"*

All Cavazos could do was laugh. Schwarzkopf had figured out what the holiday lighting at Fort Stewart would cost and had paid for it out of his own pocket.

* Rebecca Stefoff, *Norman Schwarzkopf.* Broomall, PA: Chelsea House Publishers, 1992, p. 73.

at Fort Stewart was over and he was reassigned to the Pentagon once again. He remained at a desk job at the Pentagon for one year, then was transferred in June 1986 for a second stint at Fort Lewis, Washington, as the commander of I Corps. The following month, he was promoted to lieutenant general and received his third star. That year marked his thirtieth year of military service since his graduation from West Point. Schwarzkopf was beginning to consider retirement. As he later wrote,

> I'd already endured four stints in Washington [D.C.]— more than was healthy for anybody but a politician. Moreover, at fifty-two, I'd now been in the military thirty years and had reached the age when most generals retire. Having made it back to the Pacific Northwest, I felt ready to put down roots. If the Army had let me serve out my three years at I Corps and then said it had nothing more for me to do, I'm sure I'd have retired happily. I'd probably be living in Oregon or Washington state to this day, catching a hell of a lot of salmon.[93]

Retirement remained elusive, however. Schwarzkopf was only commander of Fort Lewis for 14 months. When he moved back to the Pentagon in August 1987, it was as the army's deputy chief of staff, as well as the senior army member of the U.S. Military Staff Committee at the United Nations (UN). In some ways, this secondary role put him in situations similar to what his father had experienced while stationed in Iran. He was constantly meeting with foreign representatives, which required him to keep his diplomatic skills well honed.

The following year—1988—Schwarzkopf received his fourth star, and yet another assignment as commander-in-chief of U.S. Central Command, in Tampa, Florida. Once again, he moved his family. The children were growing up.

Cynthia had already graduated from high school, Jessica was a junior in high school, and Christian was 11 years old. It was early in his assignment at Central Command that Schwarzkopf announced—"after 32 years in the army and 25 postings on three continents"[94]—that he intended to retire at the mandatory 35 years for his rank. With three years of active duty remaining, he anticipated riding out his military tenure with little fanfare. He could not have been more wrong.

"They've Crossed the Border"

In August 1988, just three months before General Norman Schwarzkopf was assigned as commander-in-chief of U.S. Central Command in Tampa, Saddam Hussein, the autocratic leader of Iraq, ended his eight-year-long war with Iran. The war had crippled the Iraqi economy. Hussein became fixated on his neighbors, nearly all of which were oil-producing states with Arab populations. To Saddam, these nations of the Persian Gulf—Saudi Arabia, Kuwait, Oman, Yemen, and the United Arab Emirates—were responsible for his country's economic problems, despite the fact that several Arab nations had given his country billions of dollars in aid during the Iran-Iraq War. According to the Iraqi leader, the Gulf states were

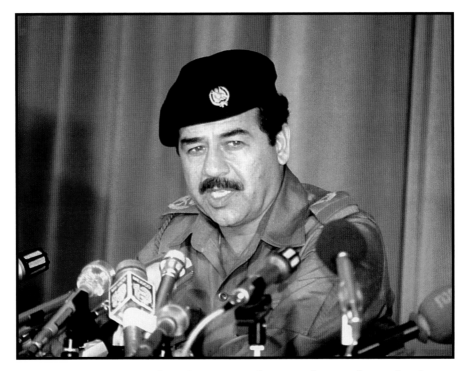

Saddam Hussein, seen here in a 1980 photograph, was determined to improve the Iraqi economy by taking control of the oil industry in nearby nations, including Kuwait.

over-producing oil, driving prices down, which was destroying his own oil-based economy.

As the powerful, volatile Saddam focused on the Gulf states, he realized that he had an army of more than one million troops, many of them experienced from the Iraq-Iran War, and that his neighbors would be easy prey. He paid particular attention to his neighbor to the south-east—Kuwait. Saddam calculated that, if he succeeded in invading and annexing Kuwait, he would control a significant portion of the available oil in the Middle East, and would increase his country's coastline from 37 to 225 miles (60 to 362 kilometers). Without question, by the late 1980s, Saddam Hussein was the wild card in the volatile geopolitics of the Middle East.

At his new posting at Central Command, Schwarzkopf became part of a Defense Department command designed to monitor and coordinate the ability of America's military forces to deploy to potential hot spots around the world, including Northern Africa and several Middle Eastern nations, including Iran, Iraq, Jordan, Saudi Arabia, and other Persian Gulf nations. In 1988, Schwarzkopf did not consider Saddam Hussein the most significant threat to the stability of the Middle East. Instead, he believed that the Soviet Union was the nation to watch, since the Soviets had been working to gain allies in the region for decades, always intent on gaining access to a warm-water port. As for Iraq, in 1988, Schwarzkopf felt that Saddam Hussein represented only a "potential threat."[95]

Because of the potential for greater Soviet influence, Schwarzkopf came to believe that the United States needed to work on developing stronger ties with the nations of the Persian Gulf region. By 1989, he had visited Kuwait to strengthen the friendship between his country and Iraq's neighbor. He attended a formal dinner dressed in the traditional Arab dishdasha robe. He made three visits to the Middle East that year, sitting down with Arab leaders playing the role of diplomat more than military commander. In October, he made a visit to the largest oil-producing nation in the entire Arab world, Saudi Arabia. He met with Arab leaders and the American ambassador, Charles W. Freeman, Jr. Discussions focused on the threat Iraq posed to its Arab neighbors.

Through his work with Central Command, General Schwarzkopf, by 1990, changed his opinion about the greatest potential threat to the Arab world of the Middle East. The Soviet Union had fallen on hard times. It was struggling with internal political changes that, by the following year, brought about its complete collapse and an end to more than 70 years of Communist control. Iraq had been pushed to the top of Schwarzkopf's list of potential threats to the stability of the Middle East. There appeared to be every possibility that Saddam Hussein might invade Kuwait and, by doing so, threaten the stability of the Saudi regime. In February, Schwarzkopf addressed the Senate Armed Services Committee and expressed these same concerns. He stated that such influence wielded by Iraq could lead to "a regional war which threatens American lives and vital U.S. interests."[96]

That summer, Schwarzkopf received information from the Central Intelligence Agency (CIA), including satellite photographs that indicated the Iraqis were massing military hardware and troops on their border with Kuwait. The same information was delivered to President George H. W. Bush, who ordered it to be passed on to the Kuwaitis. Few people took the information seriously, believing that Saddam only intended to use the troops as leverage to gain what he wanted from his neighbors.

Schwarzkopf, however, believed that Saddam might actually attack Kuwait. On July 17, Saddam had threatened Kuwait and the United Arab Emirates, saying these countries had driven "'a poisoned dagger' into Iraq's back by exceeding production quotas set by OPEC" (the Oil Producing and Exporting Countries).[97] Schwarzkopf organized Central Command's annual computer war games program, Internal Look 90, based on an Iraqi invasion of Kuwait. The games were intended to determine whether Central Command had the capacity, resources, and personnel to respond adequately and quickly to such an invasion before it was completed. The scenario-based program ran until July 28.

Just four days later, Iraqi troops and tanks crossed the border into Kuwait. Schwarzkopf received word at his home after working out on his exercise bike. The phone call came from the chairman of the Joint Chiefs of Staff, Colin Powell.

"You were right," said Powell in a calm voice. "They've crossed the border."[98]

Schwarzkopf responded confidently: "I really thought they would."[99] Schwarzkopf did not even take time to change out of his exercise clothes before rushing to Central Command headquarters.

As intelligence reports came in, it became apparent that Saddam had gone beyond even the general's expectations. Schwarzkopf had assumed that the Iraqi leader would occupy the Rumaila oil fields, which the Iraqis and Kuwaitis shared, but the Iraqi army had actually advanced all the way into the Kuwaiti capital of Kuwait City.

Fortunately, Schwarzkopf's expectations had led him to design the war games around a potential Iraqi invasion of its neighbor. He was able to begin implementing Internal Look 90 in real life almost immediately. Schwarzkopf became the focus of the American military response and Powell ordered him to Washington, D.C., to meet with the National Security Council and President George H.W. Bush.

Saddam's advance into Kuwait had been swift. The occupation had only taken a day. Saddam had annexed Kuwait right away, declaring it an Iraqi province. There was a general panic among the Kuwaiti people, thousands of whom fled into Saudi Arabia. Those who could not make it out in time "were subjected to brutal atrocities or suffered from food shortages."[100] Thousands of foreigners, including 3,000 U.S. citizens were trapped in Kuwait, as well.

As Schwarzkopf, Powell, and others examined the developing situation in Kuwait, there was great concern about Saddam's next move. With the occupation of Kuwait, he had gained control of more than 27 percent of all Middle Eastern oil facilities, which he could use as a weapon against any industrialized nation that depended on Arab oil. Intelligence reports indicated that Iraqi

Saddam Hussein's forces invaded Kuwait with lightning speed in 1990. Even after the operation began, the Iraqis worked hard to give their troops the best training possible. Here, an Iraqi military leader shouts out encouragement to his men during a training exercise.

troops were turning south toward the Saudi Arabian border. Schwarzkopf proposed that a force of 200,000 American troops be deployed to Saudi Arabian soil to keep Saddam at bay. He informed his superiors that a much larger force would be needed to drive the Iraqis out of Kuwait altogether. Powell strongly suggested to Bush that he should take a firm stand. Less than a week after Iraqi tanks rolled into the streets of Kuwait City, Schwarzkopf had been dispatched to the Saudi capital of Jidda, carrying a strategy that would unite his country and the giant Arab nation—Operation Desert Shield.

The first potential obstacle to the plan was whether King Fahd would agree to open his Islamic nation to hundreds of thousands of American troops. On August 6, a meeting was held at the king's palace with Secretary of Defense Dick Cheney; the American ambassador to Saudi Arabia, Charles Freeman; and General Schwarzkopf, who had an audience with the Saudi leader. At one point during the two-and-a-half hour session, Cheney informed Fahd that Schwarzkopf would brief him on his plan for military support:

> I showed the king a series of photos of Iraqi tanks at the Saudi border. Actually, a couple of the photos showed tanks that were *across* the Saudi border. . . . Then I outlined our plan to defend the kingdom. I didn't elaborate as to how such a deployment could actually defeat an attack—my main message was the scale of the operation, to make sure the king understood that we were talking about flooding his airfields, harbors, and military bases with tens of thousands more Americans than Saudi Arabia had ever seen.[101]

After Schwarzkopf finished his presentation and Secretary of Defense Dick Cheney spoke, the king agreed to their request.

The United States wasted no time moving its forces into the field to meet the Iraqi threat against the Saudi kingdom. The following day, American fighter planes had arrived at bases along Saudi Arabia's east coast. On August 8, President Bush announced on television that 50,000 American service personnel were being sent to Saudi Arabia to defend one of the United States' Middle Eastern allies. As for Schwarzkopf, he had already returned to the Florida.

Saddam Hussein's incursion into Kuwait had already

brought major implications for Iraq. By August 6, the UN Security Council had voted to place significant sanctions on Iraq, seriously restricting its trade with the outside world, as well as a ban on weapons to the rogue nation. President Bush began a months-long campaign of lining up allies to form a solid front in opposition to the aggression of Saddam Hussein. In all, 32 countries joined the United States in a coalition: Afghanistan, Argentina, Australia, Bahrain, Bangladesh, Belgium, Canada, Czechoslovakia, Denmark, Egypt, France, Germany, Great Britain, Greece, Italy, Kuwait, Morocco, the Netherlands, New Zealand, Niger, Norway, Oman, Pakistan, Poland, Qatar, Saudi Arabia, Senegal, South Korea, Spain, Syria, Turkey, and the United Arab Emirates.

Schwarzkopf was destined to be the man in the middle. No one was in a better position to organize the world's military response against the Iraqi leader. The 24th infantry division (mechanized), which Schwarzkopf had commanded from 1983 to 1985, was one of the units called up for service.

As U.S. naval vessels were loaded with equipment, ammunition, fuel, and troops, the logistics of transporting it all over 8,000 miles (12,875 kilometers) away to Saudi Arabia became apparent to Schwarzkopf. Even as he remained on top of the developing defensive force, however, Schwarzkopf did not become too entangled with the minor details of deployment. It was part of his style of command. He had learned years earlier "to be a leader who gives considerable leeway to the commanders he trusts and respects. That trust has to be earned, but, once earned, it is generous."[102]

By September 1, just a month after Saddam's incursion into Kuwait, 100,000 American troops were in Saudi Arabia, and tens of thousands more were en route. Through the months that followed, there were more than 675,000 combatants involved in the coalition forces sent to the Middle East, and Schwarzkopf was their commander. This number was greater than had ever served in Vietnam at any one time, and constituted the largest accumulation of field troops in an international conflict spot since World War II.

American-Saudi Culture Clash

Once the Saudi king agreed to allow thousands of American forces to establish bases on his soil to face the threat of Saddam Hussein, problems soon developed as two extremely different cultures came into close contact. Nearly everyone in Saudi Arabia practiced the Islamic faith, a conservative religion that placed many moral restrictions on activities. Even something as ordinary as women military personnel driving U.S. trucks created a problem for the Saudis, whose laws did not allow women to drive. Keenly aware of the culture clash, Schwarzkopf issued General Order #1 during the early days of Desert Shield.

The military directive noted that "Islamic law and Arabic customs prohibit or restrict certain activities which are generally permissible in Western societies."* One activity banned among American troops was the consumption of alcoholic beverages, since Islamic law forbids the use of alcohol.

Clothing was another touchy issue. Despite the raging desert heat, American forces were not permitted to wear shorts or even short sleeves. For a while, the Saudis tried to make all American women in the country wear the type of robes worn by Saudi women, which cover the wearer from head to toe. To keep cross-cultural contact to a minimum, the military did not allow its personnel to visit the Saudi capital of Riyadh.

Deliveries of some magazines and other publications to U.S. troops were also banned. Especially insulting to the Saudis were materials that had sexual content. Although this mainly included men's magazines, General Order #1 also restricted "body-building magazines, swimsuit editions of periodicals, lingerie or underwear advertisements and catalogues."**

* Jack Anderson and Dale Van Atta, *Stormin' Norman: An American Hero.* New York: Kensington Publishing, 1991, p. 163.

** Roger Cohen and Claudio Gatti, *In the Eye of the Storm: The Life of General H. Norman Schwarzkopf.* New York: Farrar, Straus and Giroux, 1991, p. 227.

Now Schwarzkopf held the most extraordinary command of his entire career. As for his family, Schwarzkopf's departure in late August was an anxious, emotional moment. He explained to his children that he was leaving soon "on an important mission that should be a source of pride to them."[103] When they asked him what he might want for Christmas, he thought for a moment, then said with regret, "Well, I might not be home for Christmas."[104]

Schwarzkopf flew out of Tampa on August 25 and arrived in the Saudi Arabian capital of Riyadh the next day. His headquarters were established in the Saudi Ministry of Defense and Aviation building, part of a heavily protected compound. From there, Schwarzkopf directed the U.S. military's efforts to protect Saudi Arabia and prepare for Kuwait's liberation. There were 16 telephones in his war room in the Saudi ministry bunker. One was wired to Joint Chiefs of Staff Chairman Colin Powell. Another went directly to President Bush.

Schwarzkopf was in Saudi Arabia just a few days before he took a helicopter over to the eastern coast to Dhahran, near the Saudi oil fields, where most of the American troops were stationed. The situation was chaotic at best. Some of the troops were housed in warehouses at the neighboring port town of Ad Dammām. At this desert base, Schwarzkopf greeted the soldiers of the 24th division, one of his old command units, which had reached Saudi Arabia on August 23, as well as the 101st airborne and the 82nd, with its nine parachute infantry battalions. Five battalions of marines were also in country. The troops Schwarzkopf surveyed were hardly prepared to engage the Iraqis if they chose to cross into Saudi Arabia. The units had almost no tanks yet and they were armed with "little more than their personal weapons, hand grenades, and some anti-tank rockets."[105] Had Saddam chosen to launch an assault onto Saudi soil

During the months before the start of the Persian Gulf War, Norman Schwarzkopf became a common sight on American television. Dressed in his desert fatigues, he gave press conferences and kept the public up to date on the progress of the military operation.

during the final week of August, he might have brought about a humiliating American defeat.

The visit from General Schwarzkopf was a huge morale booster for the troops. Their commander was with them, not a great distance from the potential battlefield. He walked among the troops, shaking hands and giving them encouragement. He even gave them fatherly hugs, showing his concern for their safety.

Over the following weeks and months, Schwarzkopf, from his headquarters in Riyadh, settled into a grueling routine of command:

> From the time of his arrival on August 26, he worked seven days a week, often putting in fifteen-hour days, beginning with staff meetings at 7 A.M. and continuing well into the evening. He ate in the War Room and slept no more than four to five hours a night. Every day, he talked to Powell, usually in the midafternoon. There was unity of purpose between them: they were running the show. In Defense Secretary Cheney and the President they found two civilians equally committed to avoiding political micro-management of the battlefield. As Cheney said on September 12, 1990, "The President belongs to what I call the "Don't-screw-around school of military strategy."[106]

Through September, more troops arrived, and coastal installations were soon stacked with American military supplies delivered by ships. Giant military aircraft, including C-130 Hercules transports and C-5A/B Galaxy cargo planes, brought in enormous quantities of everything that Schwarzkopf's troops needed to live and fight in the desert. The 24th division's M1A1 tanks reached their Saudi destinations in the closing days of the month.

As the weeks went by, Americans at home remained curious about the buildup of U.S. and coalition troops. On television, viewers in the United States became accustomed to seeing General Schwarzkopf, who held frequent press conferences. He was there, on television, dressed "in desert camouflage battle fatigues, wearing black metal generals' stars on his collar and a wristwatch on both wrists so that he could tell local time and Washington, D.C., time. . . ."[107]

Schwarzkopf received tremendous help from the Saudi commander, Lieutenant General Khalid Bin Sultan bin Abdul Aziz, a nephew of King Fahd. Early on, Khalid was not positive about the presence of American troops on his country's soil, but he soon became friendly with Schwarzkopf, and the two men worked side by side. Khalid had a great command of the English language, and he was a valuable go-between for the American commander in dealing with the Arab forces, including those from Egypt, Syria, Kuwait, Oman, Bahrain, Qatar, and the United Arab Emirates. Other nations, such as Pakistan, with a large percentage of Islamic troops, were also placed directly under the Saudi general's command.

Throughout the final months of 1990, Schwarzkopf amassed hundreds of thousands of troops and anxiously held the line against any potential Iraqi invasion of Saudi Arabia. Although the Iraqis made few overtures toward their giant Arab neighbor to the south, Schwarzkopf remained optimistic, even hopeful that the political leaders of various nations around the world and the UN would bring Saddam to their way of thinking through the economic boycott the UN had placed on Iraq. The general was in no hurry to go to war, even though he had sized up his Iraqi opponent, Saddam, as "a stubborn, cunning, but extremely limited man, used to getting his way by force and ill equipped to gauge the resolve of a world in which he had scarcely traveled."[108]

In one television interview, Schwarzkopf described his opinions about Saddam:

> I don't admire Saddam Hussein. I have absolute—I guess I would say I have great disdain for the man. I certainly have no respect for his moral or ethical principles. I have no respect for him as a military leader. He's not a military leader. He's not a military leader by any stretch of the

In the early months of 1991, American and allied forces prepared for a possible ground war against the Iraqi forces. Here, a column of U.S. marines moves across the desert landscape of Saudi Arabia, getting into position in the event that they might be needed for an offensive strike on Iraq.

imagination. All he is is a terrorist. He's a terrorist with a military force he's using for terror. And do I hate him? No, I don't hate anybody. A very great man one time said, "Love thy enemies." And that's not a bad piece of advice. But, you know, you can love them—but by God, that doesn't mean we're not going to fight them![109]

As early as mid-September, Schwarzkopf had begun to develop a military plan to remove Saddam from Kuwait. He knew he would need to utilize a massive strike force against Saddam's Republican Guard inside Kuwait. In addition to the 100,000 Iraqi troops Saddam had sent into Kuwait on August 2, the Iraqi dictator had, by the end of September, more than 430,000 soldiers in Kuwait. By the end of October, Schwarzkopf commanded no more than

200,000 troops in Saudi Arabia, who would be expected to face an Iraqi force of more than twice their number.

By October, to meet the increase in Saddam's strength, Schwarzkopf called for "more aircraft carriers, more armored divisions, and more Marine Corps." [110] By November, he entered into a second stage of building up coalition forces, especially American. The Pentagon allowed Schwarzkopf's forces to be doubled to 400,000. On the diplomatic front, by November 29, U.S. Secretary of State James Baker was able to get the UN Security Council to approve Resolution 678, which authorized coalition troops to use force against Saddam by January 15, the date Schwarzkopf himself had targeted as the soonest he would have all his forces and supplies in place for a fully operational offensive against the Iraqis.

As Schwarzkopf studied his timetable, his available fighting force, and the position of Saddam's troops in Kuwait and Iraq, he refined his strategy. While Saddam had spent months "pouring troops into the Kuwaiti sandbox," General Schwarzkopf had focused on the ground to the west of these Iraqi forces, a large, "exposed, empty western flank." [111] Rather than exclusively attack the Iraqis in Kuwait, Schwarzkopf believed he could dispatch troops in a wide "three-hundred-mile [483-kilometer] flanking move," [112] one that could help keep coalition casualties to a minimum but would require a greater amount of planning and logistical support. Schwarzkopf's strategy was complicated, large in scope, multidirectional, and well conceived:

> All the basic elements of the campaign were there. Way out
> to the west . . . was the XVIII Airborne Corps, sweeping
> around behind the Iraqi lines and cutting off the Euphrates
> River valley. To the east of the XVIII Corps was the
> VII Corps, surging into Iraq closer to Kuwait's western
> border . . . and then wheeling eastward into Kuwait itself

and attacking the Republican Guard in the north of the country. Closer to the Persian Gulf, moving directly over the Iraqi minefields and on toward Kuwait City, were the 1st and 2nd Marine expeditionary Forces and the Arab forces. In the Gulf itself was the coalition's massive naval power, preparing a possible amphibious assault, although, in General Schwarzkopf's mind, there was already the growing thought that this would probably end up as no more than a feint. The much-publicized . . . rehearsal for an amphibious landing, which began five days later on November 15, would set the Iraqis up for this deception.[113]

Schwarzkopf even had his own name for the planned campaign, although Desert Sword had been the name considered for weeks prior. He called his offensive "Desert Storm."

"Our Cause Is Just"

Although Schwarzkopf's plan looked straightforward on paper, a simple matter of deploying the right troops at the right place at the right time, the logistics were extremely complicated. To move just one corps, the XVIII for example, would involve a Herculean effort of planning and supply:

> In effect, General Schwarzkopf was asking the XVIII Corps to move 117,844 personnel, 22,884 wheeled vehicles, and 5,145 tracked vehicles an average of 530 miles [853 kilometers] down a single road from their defensive to their pre-attack positions in the space of about fourteen days. With the men and women and the vehicles would have to go more than 6 million MREs . . . , over

On Thanksgiving, 1990, President George H.W. Bush (right) visited the American forces in the Persian Gulf region. While giving the troops a much-needed morale boost, Bush also met with General Schwarzkopf (left) to discuss the latest information about the Iraqi invasion of Kuwait.

13 million gallons of water, over 23 million gallons of fuel, and over 15,000 short tons of ammunition. No army in the history of warfare had ever moved so much so far so fast.[114]

Despite these obstacles, the plan was well developed and could be implemented. It came as a result of Schwarzkopf's deep study of both the immediate threat posed by the Iraqis and their leader, as well as general military history. It was a strategy based on deception. Schwarzkopf "used dummy tanks, trucks, guns, and even a fake oil pipeline to suggest that Allied power was being concentrated to the south when in fact the main assault was to come from the north."[115]

On Thanksgiving, President Bush came to Saudi Arabia to visit the troops. With both Bush and Schwarzkopf assuming that the coalition would have to invade Kuwait to force out the Iraqis, the president asked how long the shortest possible ground war might be. The general told his commander-in-chief that three days would be the best scenario; at worst, a protracted conflict that dragged on for months, possibly ending in stalemate.

Through December, Schwarzkopf remained busy dealing with the continual details of command, including giving interviews and holding press conferences. Christmas was approaching and many of his troops, himself included, were homesick, being so far away from their families for the holidays. During an interview, Schwarzkopf expressed his feelings about being away from home. He said, "When I'm in front of the troops . . . they don't want a general to cry and that's very important to me and so therefore I won't."[116]

On January 12, the U.S. Congress authorized a war with Iraq. Three days later, Saddam completely ignored the UN's January 15 deadline for withdrawal from Kuwait. That day, President Bush signed an official National Security Directive, authorizing the use of military force against Iraq. Schwarzkopf received the directive early on the morning of January 16, 1991. Schwarzkopf called his forces into combat, sending out a message to his troops:

> I have seen in your eyes a fire of determination to get this job done quickly so we may all return to the shores of our great nation. My confidence in you is total. The President, the Congress, the American people, and indeed the world stand united in their support of your action. Our cause is just! Now you must be the thunder and lightning of Desert Storm. May God be with you, your loved ones at home, and our country.[117]

Then, on January 17, Schwarzkopf gave the orders that opened the hostilities of the Persian Gulf War.

As the war began, it was an air war, not an infantry fight. During the first 24 hours of Schwarzkopf's offensive, his coalition forces (mostly American airmen flying

As the Persian Gulf War opened, it was fought by aircraft like this F-117A Stealth bomber, rather than by ground troops. The air attack was so successful that when ground troops did enter the combat, the Iraqi forces had already been considerably weakened.

American warplanes) launched more than 1,000 flights, called sorties, against enemy targets, including the Iraqi capital of Baghdad. The Americans had at their disposal the greatest array of technologically advanced weaponry on earth, including B-52 bombers, A-10 attack bombers, F-117A Stealth bombers, and helicopters, such as the Apache with its arsenal of laser-guided missiles. Some of the American equipment jammed enemy radar, making incoming coalition planes invisible to the Iraqis. The Americans also used the latest missiles, including Tomahawk missiles with a cruising speed of nearly 900 miles (1,448 kilometers) an hour, which could be launched from the safety of a distant ship. Patriot missiles aimed at Iraqi Scud missiles that were launched at both Saudi Arabia and Israel, blasted the enemy projectiles out of the sky. In addition to the American firepower, planes from several coalition countries—notably Great Britain, Canada, France, Italy, and Saudi Arabia—performed well, augmenting the success of the Americans. The effectiveness of the air sorties was clear from the beginning. Within two weeks of the opening of the air war, Iraq's ability to coordinate the elements of war had been severely damaged. Saddam's centralized air defense was in shambles.

Much of Saddam's direct response to Schwarzkopf's offensive involved the launching of his Scud missiles. The name "Scud" was a code name for SS-1 surface-to-surface missiles Saddam had received from the Soviet Union. The Scud was an unreliable weapon, inaccurate and incapable of narrow targeting. Even so, Scuds could devastate a general-ized target, such as a mass of troops. During the first 48 hours of the coalition air assault, Saddam's forces launched eight Scuds, seven targeted at Israel and one at Saudi Arabia. The eighth Scud was shot down in flight by an American-launched Patriot missile. During the entire Persian Gulf War, 81 Iraqi Scuds were launched. Patriots shot down several of them, prompting Saudi Arabian shops in Riyadh and Dhahran to begin selling Scud-versus-Patriot T-shirts. During the following six weeks, Schwarzkopf's air forces launched more than 100,000 sorties over Iraq, destroying nearly all of Saddam's Air Force. The Iraqis accumulated tens of thousands of casualties, with some estimates running as high as 50,000. Allied casualties were miniscule.

After the first five weeks of aerial bombing, President Bush gave Saddam an opportunity to withdraw his forces from Kuwait, which the Iraqi leader ignored. It was now February 24, and the president ordered Schwarzkopf to send in ground forces. Schwarzkopf, however, had already sent troops secretly into Iraq as early as the first day of aerial bombing back on January 17. Those forces were already in position in the middle of Iraq.

On February 24, the coalition forces could officially make their presence known to the enemy as they began to move in a region where Hussein was at his weakest, his highly neglected right flank. Other coalition troops, including U.S.

marines, Saudi forces, and units from various Arab countries, broke across the Kuwaiti-Iraqi border in a straight advance toward Kuwait City.

Almost immediately, Saddam's ground forces faced a highly organized tide of thousands of coalition troops, who were backed by heavy air support, including warplanes and attack helicopters. Although the Iraqi army in the field may have numbered as high as one million by February, it proved no match for the well-armed multinational force. Tens of thousands of Iraqi soldiers surrendered, putting up no fight at all. In fact, the Iraqis were surrendering so quickly and in such large numbers that Schwarzkopf pushed forward his timetable for sending his various units into their combat roles, intent on forcing the enemy to give up as quickly as possible and to ensure that each coalition unit was able to participate in the fight.

One key to the quick success of the coalition's offensive was its speed and the element of surprise. Coalition units sometimes moved 50 miles (81 kilometers) into enemy territory before they encountered even a single enemy combatant. By the end of the second day of the ground war, Schwarzkopf asked about the number of coalition casualties. A subordinate officer told him they were low. When the general asked how low, he was informed: "One report of one wounded soldier, sir." Schwarzkopf was ecstatic.[118]

For the coalition forces, the casualties remained low, and the territorial advances were significant. U.S. marines advanced toward Kuwait City and the Marine 1st division fought for control of the city's international airport against the Iraqi 3rd division, which proved no match. To the west, the XVIII Corps reached the Euphrates Valley, and the 24th infantry division captured air bases at Tallil and Jaliba after meeting resistance from the Iraqi 49th division. The 24th advanced along Highway 8, a ten-lane thoroughfare that led straight to the Iraqi city of Basra. Other coalition

After the ground offensive began, Iraqi soldiers, like this column of captured troops, were quickly captured. As more and more Iraqis surrendered or became prisoners, Saddam Hussein's forces lacked the strength to fight off the American and allied onslaught.

fighting units, especially American forces, met Iraqi units in the field and defeated them quickly, destroying hundreds of Iraqi tanks along the way.

After only four days of the ground war, the Iraqis were ready to negotiate the terms of their surrender. By then, Arab coalition forces had been allowed to enter Kuwait City under Schwarzkopf's orders. Three out of every four Iraqi divisions (29 of 42) had been defeated and "rendered completely ineffective."[119] Ninety percent of Iraq's 4,000 tanks in the field had been destroyed. Close to 70,000 prisoners had been taken. Only 100 hours after the launching of General Schwarzkopf's ground war plan, the enemy was utterly routed and Kuwait was liberated.

Even as the bulk of the Iraqi military in the field surrendered to coalition forces, though, Saddam's forces set fire to Kuwaiti oil fields as they retreated back to their homeland. Several hundred oil wells were set afire, burning uncontrollably and filled the sky with "huge, dense plumes of oily smoke high into the atmosphere."[120] When Schwarzkopf viewed the punitive, wholesale destruction of Kuwait by the Iraqis, he was stunned: "I was totally unprepared for the scene, and the first thing that flashed through my mind was that if I ever visualized what hell would look like, this was it."[121]

Less than one week after the end of the ground war, on March 3, 1991, Schwarzkopf met with Iraqi commanders and government officials, along with coalition commanders from Saudi Arabia, Kuwait, Great Britain, and France, in a tent at the Iraqi airfield in Safwan. Here, the Iraqis were allowed to surrender and they accepted coalition terms, which included acceptance of the UN resolutions, the agreement that no Iraqi aircraft could fly in Iraqi airspace where coalition forces are located.

The Persian Gulf War came to an end as abruptly as it had been fought. Schwarzkopf reveled in the coalition's casualty figures. Eighteen coalition planes had been shot down, even though the Iraqis claimed to have shot down nearly 200. From February 24 to 27, 155 U.S. military personnel were killed, a number much lower than any military expert, including Schwarzkopf himself, had predicted. (During Desert Shield, an additional 108 had been killed.) The unit casualty list was nearly infinitesimal. The XVIII airborne division placed nearly 118,000 combatants in the Persian Gulf conflict. Of those, twenty-one were killed, and an additional 62 wounded. One mobile military hospital had prepared to handle 1,200 casualties a day, but never saw more than 76 patients. The lack of fighting tenacity on the part of the Iraqis was an important reason for the low casualty figures, but it was the general's unwillingness to sacrifice his forces unnecessarily that helped keep casualties low as well.

9

Epilogue

Despite having concluded the military aspect of the Persian Gulf mission by the end of February 1991, Schwarzkopf did not return to the United States until April. He wanted to help make certain that many of his troops found their way home first. (More than 200,000 of them returned before he did.) Through these months, the majority of his troops remained in Saudi Arabia or Kuwait, helping to restore order to a devastated corner of the world.

Schwarzkopf had struggled with the sense of lacking a purpose when he had gone to Vietnam, especially during his second tour 20 years earlier. Even when he went to Grenada in the early 1980s, he had asked himself hard questions about

After the publication of his autobiography, *It Doesn't Take a Hero*, in 1993, Schwarzkopf spent some time promoting the book, which subsequently became a best-seller.

the value of the mission to restore independence to a tiny island nation in the Caribbean. His Persian Gulf experiences, on the other hand, needed no reassurances. He had commanded a massive force with a clear mandate from the international community to brand Saddam Hussein as a ruthless dictator and aggressor and to remove his army from Kuwait. In this, Schwarzkopf had succeeded.

Although he spoke many times about the war as a victory for every man and woman who had participated in it, the accolades still fell to him from every direction. While he was still in Saudi Arabia in March, the French embassy in Riyadh gave him a general's sword and the

French Foreign Legion's white kepi (military cap). The Saudis, who had faced the threat of Saddam Hussein directly, were among the most grateful, and they presented Schwarzkopf with a very unique honor. He was decorated with the Order of King Abdul Aziz, First Class, which had never before been granted to any non-Saudi. At the ceremony, held in Riyadh just before the general prepared to leave Saudi Arabia, General Khalid spoke admiringly of his friend and colleague: "The American troops who came to Saudi Arabia were inspired by General Schwarzkopf's example and by their own instincts for fairness. . . . I have often said that if the world is to have a superpower, thank God it is the United States!"[122]

Even with Schwarzkopf's planned retirement just months away, Joint Chiefs of Staff Chairman Powell offered Schwarzkopf the post of chief of staff of the army. The general politely turned the offer down, insisting that the war had not changed his mind to leave the military in August 1991.

When he finally left the Middle East in April, Schwarzkopf boarded a military plane bound for Tampa, Florida, where he would be reunited with his family. The general had spent nearly 35 years in uniform, and he was returning to his country as a war hero. His name had become a household word. He was as famous in his day as General Ulysses S. Grant had been during the Civil War, General John J. Pershing during World War I, or General George Patton during World War II. On his return, he found that American children were collecting bubblegum cards featuring those involved in the Persian Gulf War, including President Bush, General Powell, Dick Cheney, and, of course, General Schwarzkopf. He had returned from war on three previous occasions, twice from Vietnam and once from Grenada. The greetings he received then were nothing compared to the welcome he experienced in the spring of 1991:

> A brass band and a crowd of well-wishers greeted him when he stepped off the plane at MacDill Air Force Base in Tampa, Florida. With tears in his eyes, he wrapped his family in a bear hug, listened to the national anthem, and declared, "It's a great day to be a soldier."[123]

When Schwarzkopf arrived at his home, he and his family celebrated the Christmas he had missed eight months earlier. He was shocked to find his dining room filled with presents from people around the world who wanted to thank him for his efforts in the Persian Gulf War. The next day, he and his family spent time in their garage, which was stacked with "hundreds of different kinds of teddy bears, ranging from small creatures to five-foot giants. . . . There was also a big bronze sculpture of a bear fishing."[124] Schwarzkopf donated most of the toy bears to hospitals and children's homes.

Other, more lavish honors also awaited the returning soldier. He was thanked by President Bush in a speech to Congress. He received the Presidential Medal of Freedom. The following month, Schwarzkopf received an honorary knighthood from British Queen Elizabeth II.

Schwarzkopf paid one more official visit to the Middle East, stopping in Egypt, Kuwait, and Saudi Arabia. Then, at summer's end, on August 30, 1991, General H. Norman Schwarzkopf quietly retired, having served his country since his graduation from West Point in 1956.

In retirement, Schwarzkopf remained a popular figure. He and Brenda stayed in the Tampa area. Republicans discussed the possibility of the former general running for president of the United States. He declined. As his sister Sally said in an interview, "Norm hates politics."[125]

Schwarzkopf has remained in the public eye through his work with the media, speaking engagements, and various foundation organizations. In 1993, he published his autobiography, *It Doesn't Take a Hero*, which became a best-seller. He worked closely with the production of six critically acclaimed television specials, including *D-Day*, which won a Peabody Award. The former general has also served as a consultant for the NBC television network.

One project in which Schwarzkopf is closely involved is a foundation called "STARBRIGHT World," a private organization designed to link up on the Internet as many as 30,000 children who suffer from serious illnesses. He also helped found a Florida camp called Boggy Creek Gang, a year-round facility that provides recreation and an outdoor experiences for chronically ill children.

Since his retirement, Schwarzkopf has remained an avid outdoorsman, and fishing and hunting are still an important part of his life. He currently serves on the Nature Conservancy's President's Conservation Council and is the national spokesman for an organization called Recovery of the Grizzly Bear, a group dedicated to increasing America's grizzly bear population and preserving the bears' natural habitat.

On August 2, 2000, which marked the tenth anniversary of Saddam Hussein's incursion into Kuwait, Schwarzkopf was onboard the U.S.S. *New Jersey*, an American battleship, where he delivered an address. He spoke of his own years of military service, and of the ongoing service provided by countless troops from all branches of the military. He recalled how, as a West Point cadet, he had been reminded constantly of the academy's motto: "duty, honor, country." He also explained that "it was in the field, from the rice paddies of Southeast Asia to the sands of the Middle East" that he finally came to understand the true meaning and significance of the motto."[126] He went on to encourage his audience always to remember the "heroic dedication" of the more than half a million servicemen and women who helped bring about "that magnificent victory in the sand."[127] His words were reminiscent of those he had spoken to the troops of the XVIII Airborne Corps nearly ten years earlier as they prepared to leave Saudi soil on March 8, 1991. He had reminded them of their own personal commitment and their courage in facing the Iraqi enemy:

> Valiant charges by courageous men over 250 kilometers [155 miles] of enemy territory. Along with a force of over 1,500 tanks, almost 250 attack helicopters, over 48,500 pieces of military equipment moving around, behind, and into the enemy and totally breaking his back and defeating him in 100 hours. It's a war story worth telling, and every one of you deserves to tell it.[128]

Schwarzkopf's story, his own personal legacy, was certainly worth telling. His long military career had spanned years of tragedy for America's men and women in uniform, but had ended with the rebirth of a military that had regained its confidence, had learned the hard lessons of Vietnam, and had won a new, positive reputation among the American people. Schwarzkopf's story featured chapters rich with images of professional valor and courage; of commanding from the heart, as well as the head; of remembering the importance of family; of loyalty to one's country; and of a never-ending search for those traits that make anyone a better person.

1934	H. Norman Schwarzkopf is born in Trenton, New Jersey, on August 22.
1946	Twelve-year-old Norman moves to Tehran, Iran, to live with his father, who instructs the military police program of the shah.
1947	Schwarzkopf's family moves to Geneva, Switzerland, when Norman, Sr., is transferred by the U.S. army; Norman, Jr., attends Ecole Internationale, a private school.
1948	Schwarzkopf family moves to Frankfurt, Germany.
1949	Schwarzkopf family moves to Heidelberg, Germany.
1950–1952	Sixteen-year-old Norman, Jr., attends military school at Valley Forge Military Academy.
1952–1956	Schwarzkopf attends West Point Military Academy and graduates with the class of 1956.
1956–1957	Attends Airborne School at Fort Benning, Georgia.
1957–1959	Assigned duties in Berlin, Germany, as an aide-de-camp to Brigadier General Charles Johnson; in November 1958, Norman Schwarzkopf, Sr., dies.
1961	Returns to Fort Benning, Georgia, to attend Infantry Officers' Advanced Course.
1962–1964	Earns master's degree at the University of Southern California, Los Angeles.
1964	Accepts teaching assignment at West Point.
1965–1966	Serves a yearlong tour of duty in Vietnam.
1966–1968	Returns to his teaching post at West Point; on July 6, 1968, marries Brenda Holsinger.
1968–1969	Attends army's Command and General Staff College at Leavenworth, Kansas.
1969–1970	Returns for a second tour of duty in Vietnam; comes home disillusioned with the military and the war; in August 1970, the Schwarzkopfs have their first child, Cynthia.
1970–1972	Holds post at the Pentagon with the Officer Personnel Directorate of the infantry branch; in March 1972, the Schwarzkopfs have their second child, Jessica.
1972–1973	Attends U.S. Army College in Carlisle, Pennsylvania.
1973–1974	Reassigned to the Pentagon in the office of financial management.

1974–1976	Serves as deputy commander of Fort Richardson's 172nd infantry brigade in Anchorage, Alaska; in October 1976, Schwarzkopf's mother, Ruth, dies.
1976–1978	Serves as brigade commander, 9th infantry division, at Fort Lewis, Washington; in June 1977, Schwarzkopfs have their third child, Christian.
1978–1980	Serves as deputy with Pacific Command, in Hawaii.
1980–1982	Serves as assistant division commander, 8th mechanized infantry division, in Mainz, Germany.
1982–1983	Serves as director of military personnel management at Pentagon.
1983	Serves as commander during Grenada military operations.
1983–1985	Commander of 24th mechanized infantry division, at Fort Stewart, Georgia.
1985–1986	Assistant deputy chief of staff at Pentagon.
1986–1987	Commander, I Corps, at Fort Lewis, Washington.
1987–1988	Serves as deputy chief of staff at Pentagon.
1988–1991	Commander-in-chief of Central Command in Tampa, Florida.
1990–1991	Serves as commander of coalition forces in Persian Gulf War.
1991	In August, retires after 35 years of active military service.

CHAPTER 1

1. General H. Norman Schwarzkopf (with Peter Petre), *General H. Norman Schwarzkopf, the Autobiography: It Doesn't Take a Hero*. New York: Linda Grey, Bantam Books, 1992, p. 13.
2. Ibid., p. 7.
3. Ibid., p. 14.
4. Ibid., p. 2.
5. Ibid., p. 4.
6. Ibid., p. 3.
7. Ibid.
8. Ibid., p. 9.
9. Ibid., p. 11.
10. Ibid.
11. Ibid., p. 17.
12. Ibid., p. 18.
13. Ibid., p. 19.
14. Ibid.
15. Ibid., p. 21.
16. Ibid., p. 24.
17. Ibid.
18. Ibid., p. 25.
19. "H. Norman Schwarzkopf," *Current Biography Yearbook*. New York: H. Wilson, 1991, p. 507.

CHAPTER 2

20. General H. Norman Schwarzkopf (with Peter Petre), *General H. Norman Schwarzkopf, the Autobiography: It Doesn't Take a Hero*. New York: Linda Grey, Bantam Books, 1992, p. 15.
21. Ibid., p. 28.
22. Ibid., p. 29.
23. Ibid., p. 31.
24. Ibid., p. 32.
25. Ibid., p. 35.
26. Ibid., p. 36.
27. Ibid., p. 37.
28. Ibid., p. 41.
29. Ibid., p. 42.
30. Ibid., p. 46.
31. Ibid., p. 48.
32. Ibid.
33. Ibid., p. 51.

CHAPTER 3

34. Roger Cohen and Claudio Gatti, *In the Eye of the Storm: The Life of General H. Norman Schwarzkopf*. New York: Farrar, Straus and Giroux, 1991, p. 59.
35. Ibid., p. 60.
36. Jack Anderson and Dale Van Atta, *Stormin' Norman: An American Hero*. New York: Kensington Publishing, 1991, p. 22.

37. General H. Norman Schwarzkopf (with Peter Petre), *General H. Norman Schwarzkopf, the Autobiography: It Doesn't Take a Hero*. New York: Linda Grey, Bantam Books, 1992, p. 57.
38. Ibid., p. 58.
39. Anderson and Van Atta, p. 23.
40. Cohen and Gatti, p. 66.
41. Ibid., p. 70.
42. Schwarzkopf, p. 71.
43. Ibid., p. 72.
44. Ibid.

CHAPTER 4

45. Rebecca Stefoff, *Norman Schwarzkopf*. Broomall, PA: Chelsea House Publishers, 1992, p. 39.
46. Ibid., p. 40.
47. General H. Norman Schwarzkopf (with Peter Petre), *General H. Norman Schwarzkopf, the Autobiography: It Doesn't Take a Hero*. New York: Linda Grey, Bantam Books, 1992, p. 75.
48. Roger Cohen and Claudio Gatti, *In the Eye of the Storm: The Life of General H. Norman Schwarzkopf*. New York: Farrar, Straus and Giroux, 1991, p. 74.
49. Schwarzkopf, p. 83.
50. Cohen and Gatti, p. 75.
51. Stefoff, p. 43.
52. Cohen and Gatti, p. 77.
53. Stefoff, p. 47.
54. Schwarzkopf, p. 121.
55. Stefoff, p. 49.
56. Cohen and Gatti, p. 93.
57. Ibid., p. 94.
58. Ibid.
59. Ibid., p. 95.
60. Ibid., p. 96.
61. Schwarzkopf, p. 150.
62. Ibid., p. 153.
63. Ibid., p. 154.
64. Ibid., p. 155.
65. Stefoff, p. 14.
66. Cohen and Gatti, p. 112.
67. Stefoff, p. 59.

CHAPTER 5

68. Roger Cohen and Claudio Gatti, *In the Eye of the Storm: The Life of General H. Norman Schwarzkopf*. New York: Farrar, Straus and Giroux, 1991, p. 115.
69. General H. Norman Schwarzkopf (with Peter Petre), *General H. Norman Schwarzkopf, the Autobiography: It Doesn't Take a Hero*. New York: Linda Grey, Bantam Books, 1992, p. 176.

70. Cohen and Gatti, p. 116.
71. Ibid., p. 119.
72. Ibid., p. 128.
73. Schwarzkopf, p. 203.
74. Ibid., p. 205.
75. Cohen and Gatti, p. 139.
76. Ibid.
77. Schwarzkopf, p. 229.
78. Ibid., p. 230.
79. Cohen and Gatti, pp. 144–145.
80. Ibid., p. 145.
81. Schwarzkopf, p. 239.
82. Ibid., p. 245.

CHAPTER 6

83. Roger Cohen and Claudio Gatti, *In the Eye of the Storm: The Life of General H. Norman Schwarzkopf*. New York: Farrar, Straus and Giroux, 1991, p. 161.
84. General H. Norman Schwarzkopf (with Peter Petre), *General H. Norman Schwarzkopf, the Autobiography: It Doesn't Take a Hero*. New York: Linda Grey, Bantam Books, 1992, p. 247.
85. Cohen and Gatti, p. 163.
86. Ibid., p. 162.
87. Schwarzkopf, p. 250.
88. Ibid., p. 254.
89. Rebecca Stefoff, *Norman Schwarzkopf*. Broomall, PA: Chelsea House Publishers, 1992, p. 70.
90. Ibid., p. 71.
91. Quoted in Schwarzkopf, p. 258.
92. Ibid., p. 266.
93. Stefoff, p. 73.
94. Schwarzkopf, p. 266.

CHAPTER 7

95. Rebecca Stefoff, *Norman Schwarzkopf*. Broomall, PA: Chelsea House Publishers, 1992, p. 78.
96. Roger Cohen and Claudio Gatti, *In the Eye of the Storm: The Life of General H. Norman Schwarzkopf*. New York: Farrar, Straus and Giroux, 1991, p. 184.
97. General H. Norman Schwarzkopf (with Peter Petre), *General H. Norman Schwarzkopf, the Autobiography: It Doesn't Take a Hero*. New York: Linda Grey, Bantam Books, 1992, p. 292.
98. Ibid., p. 295.
99. Cohen and Gatti, p. 186.
100. Ibid., p. 189.
101. Schwarzkopf, p. 305.
102. Cohen and Gatti, p. 200.
103. Ibid., p. 203.

104. Ibid.
105. Ibid., p. 210.
106. Ibid., p. 216.
107. Stefoff, p. 85.
108. Schwarzkopf, p. 305.
109. Cohen and Gatti, p. 200.
110. Ibid., p. 210.
111. Ibid., p. 216.
112. Stefoff, p. 85.
113. Cohen and Gatti, p. 226.

CHAPTER 8

114. Roger Cohen and Claudio Gatti, *In the Eye of the Storm: The Life of General H. Norman Schwarzkopf*. New York: Farrar, Straus and Giroux, 1991, p. 239.
115. Ibid., p. 241.
116. Ibid., p. 248.
117. Ibid., p. 260.
118. Ibid., p. 289.
119. Ibid., p. 293.
120. Rebecca Stefoff, *Norman Schwarzkopf*. Broomall, PA: Chelsea House Publishers, 1992, p. 97.
121. Cohen and Gatti, p. 303.

CHAPTER 9

122. Roger Cohen and Claudio Gatti, *In the Eye of the Storm: The Life of General H. Norman Schwarzkopf*. New York: Farrar, Straus and Giroux, 1991, p. 315.
123. Rebecca Stefoff, *Norman Schwarzkopf*. Broomall, PA: Chelsea House Publishers, 1992, p. 104.
124. Cohen and Gatti, p. 327.
125. Ibid., p. 325.
126. www.nytimes.com/library/politics/camp/080200
127. Ibid.
128. Cohen and Gatti, pp. 310–311.

Adler, Bill. *The Generals: The New American Heroes*. New York: Avon Books, 1991.

Allen, Thomas B., et al. *War in the Gulf*. Atlanta: Turner Publishing, 1991.

Anderson, Jack, and Dale Van Atta. *Stormin' Norman: An American Hero*. New York: Kensington Publishing Corporation, 1991.

Cohen, Roger, and Claudio Gatti. *In the Eye of the Storm: The Life of General H. Norman Schwarzkopf*. New York: Farrar, Straus and Giroux, 1991.

Cohen, William A. *The New Art of the Leader: Leading With Integrity and Honor*. Paramus, NJ: Prentice Hall Press, 2000.

Connelly, Owen. *On War and Leadership: The Words of Combat Commanders From Frederick the Great to Norman Schwarzkopf*. Princeton: Princeton University Press, 2002.

Dunnigan, James, and Daniel Masterson. *The War of the Warrior: Business Tactics and Techniques From History's Twelve Greatest Generals*. New York: St. Martin's Press, 1997.

Morris, M.E. *H. Norman Schwarzkopf: Road to Triumph*. New York: St. Martin's Paperbacks, 1991.

"Norman Schwarzkopf," *Current Biography Yearbook*, 1991. New York: H. Wilson, 1991.

Pyle, Richard. *Schwarzkopf: The Man, the Mission, the Triumph*. New York: Signet Books, 1991.

Reynolds, Richard T. *Heart of the Storm: The Genesis of the Air Campaign Against Iraq*. Maxwell AFB, AL: Air University Press, 1995.

Schwarzkopf, H. Norman, with Peter Petre. *General H. Norman Schwarzkopf: The Autobiography: It Doesn't Take a Hero*. New York: Bantam Books, 1992.

Stefoff, Rebecca. *Norman Schwarzkopf*. Broomall, PA: Chelsea House Publishers, 1992.

page:

14: Courtesy of the NJ State Police Museum
17: © Bettmann/CORBIS
24: © Hulton|Archive, by Getty Images
28: © Blaine Harrington III/CORBIS
30: Courtesy of the Valley Forge Military Academy and Junior College
33: Courtesy of the Valley Forge Military Academy and Junior College
37: Courtesy of the United States Army
40: Courtesy of the United States Army
43: Courtesy of the National Archives 111-CC-74269
47: © Bettmann/CORBIS
54: Courtesy of the United States Army
57: © Bettmann/CORBIS
62: Courtesy of the United States Army
63: Courtesy of the United States Army

68: Courtesy of the U.S. Department of Defense
72: © Associated Press, AP
75: © CORBIS
77: Courtesy of the U.S. Department of Defense
83: © Associated Press, AP
87: © David Turnley/CORBIS
92: Courtesy of the United States Air Force
95: © Associated Press, U.S. Department of Defense
99: Courtesy of the George Bush Presidential Library
101: Courtesy of the U.S. Department of Defense
104: © Associated Press, AP
107: © Najlah Feanny/CORBIS SABA

Cover: Department of the Army, Office of the Chief of Public Information, Media Services Division, Washington, D.C. 20310-1507

Frontis: © Associated Press, AP

TIM McNEESE is an Associate Professor of History at York College in Nebraska. He is the author of more than fifty books and educational materials on everything from Egyptian pyramids to American Indians. Professor McNeese graduated from York College with his Associate of Arts degree, as well as Harding University where he received his Bachelor of Arts degree in history and political science. He received his Master of Arts degree in history from Southwest Missouri State University. His audiences range from elementary students to adults. He is currently in his 27th year of teaching. Professor McNeese's writing career has earned him a citation in the "Something About the Author" reference work. He is married to Beverly McNeese who teaches English at York college.

CASPAR W. WEINBERGER was the fifteenth secretary of defense, serving under President Ronald Reagan from 1981 to 1987. Born in California in 1917, he fought in the Pacific during World War II then went on to pursue a law career. He became an active member of the California Republican Party and was named the party's chairman in 1962. Over the next decade, Weinberger held several federal government offices, including chairman of the Federal Trade Commission and secretary of health, education, and welfare. Ronald Reagan appointed him to be secretary of defense in 1981.

During his years at the Pentagon, Weinberger worked to protect the United States against the Soviet Union, which many people at the time perceived as the greatest threat to America. He became one of the most respected secretaries of defense in history and served longer than any previous secretary except for Robert McNamara (who served 1961–1968). Today, Weinberger is chairman of the influential *Forbes* magazine.

EARLE RICE JR. is a former senior design engineer and technical writer in the aerospace industry. After serving nine years with the U.S. Marine Corps, he attended San Jose City College and Foothill College on the San Francisco Peninsula. He has devoted full time to his writing since 1993 and has written more than forty books for young adults. Earle is a member of the Society of Children's Book Writers and Illustrators; the League of World War I Aviation Historians and its UK-based sister organization, Cross & Cockade International, the United States Naval Institute, and the Air Force Association.